# THE DAY PEACE BROKE OUT

## THE VE-DAY EXPERIENCE

### MIKE BROWN

D1450238

SUTTON PUBLISHING

First published in 2005 by
Sutton Publishing Limited · Phoenix Mill
Thrupp · Stroud · Gloucestershire · GL5 2BU

British Library Cataloguing in Publication Data
A catalogue record for this book is available from the British Library.

ISBN 0-7509-4118-9

Typeset in 12.5pt Garamond
Typesetting and origination by
Sutton Publishing Limited.
Printed and bound in England by
J.H. Haynes & Co. Ltd, Sparkford.

# Contents

# CHAPTER 1

# *Whose Victory?*

At the time of the Munich Crisis in September 1938, popular sentiment in Britain had been heavily anti-war; cries of 'Stand by the Czechs' had been drowned out by calls for peace. When Neville Chamberlain returned from Munich promising 'Peace for our time', he received a hero's welcome, cheered by crowds at the airport, cheered by crowds at Buckingham Palace and cheered at Downing Street – where the crowd was so big that the police had trouble controlling it.

Yet public opinion, often fickle, was changing rapidly. People had been scared out of their wits, and that would not happen again. The French historian André Maurois wrote:

In January 1939 I went to Great Britain for a lecture tour that took me into all corners of the country. There I found out that public opinion was now ahead of the government. The latter was hesitating to adopt conscription; the country was energetically demanding it. Everywhere English men and women of all classes said to me, 'We must not allow this man Hitler to dominate Europe; we must have a large army and a strong air force.'

When war was declared in September 1939 Britain entered it confident of victory and, what is more, a swift victory. The BEF embarked for France to the sound of bands playing 'We're gonna hang out the washing on the Siegfried Line', a popular hit of the period. Propaganda began immediately. The press was full of pieces describing German losses and Allied advances. On 14 September, for example, the *Daily Mirror* reported:

Saarbrücken, the key German city across the River Saar, is now surrounded by French troops . . . The French advance continues. On a front of more than twenty-five miles many German villages have been captured . . . important positions, and notably some good observation posts, have been

Popular music often reflects the general sentiment of the time. This sheet music for the song 'I'm Sending You the Siegfried Line', demonstrates how, in 1939, many in Britain thought the war would be something of a walkover.

occupied . . . Heavy French tanks crashed through the German pillboxes and barbed wire entanglements. German losses, it is stated, are so great that the number of doctors and nurses available is insufficient to deal with them.

The same newspaper reported a Polish communiqué stating that, 'Polish troops had taken 1,000 German prisoners after routing a German division in the region of Kutno, west of Warsaw.'

Two days later the *Daily Mirror* announced that:

The British Navy is already driving the U-Boats off the sea . . . Hitler's troops were reported last night to be retreating from their advance positions all along the northern flank of the western front . . . Saarbrücken itself was reported . . . to have been reduced to ruins by bombardment from the Maginot forts . . . German hopes of an early peace are dwindling; rationing is tighter – even cat and dog food is rationed; the French offensive on the Western Front is causing mass evacuation of German towns.

Despite such grand claims, the result of the war in Poland was a foregone conclusion. France and Britain, having entered the war in support of Poland, were in reality able to offer little but encouragement. The Polish Army fought with great tenacity, but its German opponents were vastly superior in terms of numbers, training and equipment and, perhaps most telling of all, the Luftwaffe had established complete mastery of the air in the first few days; this it ruthlessly exploited.

On 17 September, Russia took a hand; the Red Army invaded eastern Poland. As ever, Poland was the meat sandwiched between its two great neighbours. The inevitable end came when Warsaw surrendered on the 27th; the first test of the tactics of *Blitzkrieg* ('Lightning War') was a resounding success. Hitler now laid his plans for the rest of Europe. On 9 October preparations were set in motion for 'an offensive action on the northern flank of the Western front crossing the area of Luxembourg, Belgium and Holland'.

The fall of Poland seemed to leave the war in a kind of limbo. After all, the Allies had gone to war because of the German invasion; what was now the point of continuing? On 6 October Hitler put out peace feelers through neutral countries, but public opinion both in Britain and France had swung completely since the wave of pacifism that had engulfed them in September 1938. Hitler's attack on Poland had underlined his untrustworthiness. Propaganda had proved so successful that the British and French publics had no doubt who would win. It was said, just like in 1914, that it might be 'all over by Christmas', and that this time Hitler had 'bitten off more than he could chew'. It was high time he was taught a lesson, and the Allies, safe from attack behind the massive fortifications of the Maginot Line, were just the ones to do it. On the 12th, Hitler's peace offer was rejected.

The *Daily Express* of 2 November carried an article giving the views of a Dr Rosinski:

Once again, as in 1914, the young men were off to war, and this scene of farewell was repeated up and down the country.

Very few of the leading [German] professional soldiers believe in a lightning victory. That is the pet idea of the Nazi politicians. The German generals have few hopes of being able to follow the classic German strategy of moving very rapidly so as to turn their enemies' flanks. They may not even be anxious to invade Holland or Belgium, or Switzerland to give them the chance of doing this. They are thinking . . . of frontal attacks. These are not to be decided by a sudden stroke, but by a long struggle. One side will eat away the enemy's position until he collapses . . . the Germans have lost their old pre-eminence in what is called 'the higher study of war'.

The theme of much Allied propaganda, repeatedly expressed by experts, was that the Germans did not have the stomach, and more importantly the raw materials, for a long war.

On 5 April Chamberlain made a speech that, in retrospect, seems to have been sorely tempting fate, 'After seven months of war, I feel ten times as confident of victory as I did at the beginning. Hitler has missed the bus.' He little knew that a month before, on 3 March, Hitler had ordered the invasion of Norway and Denmark. Just four days after Chamberlain's speech the Phoney War came to an abrupt end as German forces carried out their invasion plans; Denmark was a walkover, surrendering the same day, but Norway was a harder nut. It was at this time that the rest of Europe learnt a new name and a new fear. Vidkun Quisling, an extreme right-wing Norwegian politician, had been having secret meetings with German agents for some time. The original German plan had been for his supporters to seize power with some German support. A back-up plan was prepared based around surprise German troop landings; this plan soon superseded the original one, to the extent that Quisling and his supporters were kept ignorant of any details. Apart from serious losses suffered by the German Navy, the landings themselves were successful, with very little, if any, help from Quisling's supporters, but it suited all sides to claim that their part had been a vital one.

On 15 April, British troops landed in Norway. At first they had some success, but overwhelming German air superiority meant that each gain was soon followed by retreat, while Namsos, the main British base, was flattened by repeated air raids. On 2 May, Namsos was evacuated under air attack, with the loss of three destroyers and a sloop. (The last Allied forces would leave Norway in early June.) The campaign had little to commend it; both land and sea forces had proved woefully ineffective, lacking adequate air support. British confidence in the government dropped to an all-time low.

On 8 May, Chamberlain appealed to the opposition parties to join a coalition government, but it was all too late. Labour refused to join any government which he led. There followed a two-day debate in the House of Commons, where frustration with the government exploded. Leo Amery repeated Cromwell's words, this time against Chamberlain, 'You have sat too long here for any good you have been doing. Depart, I say, and let us have done with you. In the name of God, go.' And on 10 May, Chamberlain did just that. Nearly a hundred Tories defied a three-line whip, voting with the opposition, and Chamberlain resigned. His favoured successor was the Foreign Secretary, Lord Halifax, yet Halifax seemed to realise that he would not make a good war leader and refused the post. Eventually Winston Churchill was the man summoned to Buckingham Palace, to be asked to form a government.

At dawn that day, 10 May, the German Army rolled into neutral Holland, Belgium and Luxembourg in a massive attack which made the Norwegian affair seem like a side-show. Hitler had gathered eighty-nine divisions for the task, with another forty-seven in reserve. The British Expeditionary Force (BEF) entered Belgium to set up a defensive line.

*Blitzkrieg*, perfected in Poland, hit western Europe. Airborne units, dropping ahead of the main army, seized key points in the elaborate system of defensive fortifications, rendering the defences useless; Holland fell in five days. The vaunted Maginot Line, into which France had poured billions of francs, and all its hopes, was outflanked by German armour through what was thought to be the impenetrable Ardennes forest. This thrust pierced the French front line and drove on to the Channel coast west of Abbeville, cutting off most of the BEF from the main French forces to the south.

The fact that the Germans, so recently written off, were not only advancing, but at an unbelievable speed, seemed like a form of magic. And if not magic, why then, the answer must be treason. As in Norway, rumours were rife of 'fifth columnists', German sympathisers waiting for their chance to strike, with sabotage and other despicable acts, to hinder the defenders and aid the invaders. In Britain, news, first from Norway, then from the Low Countries, generated fears, almost to the level of panic, of the fifth column. In his book *Invasion 1940* Peter Fleming summed up the general paranoia, 'Flashing lights, poisoned sweets, bridges blown too soon or not at all, punctured tyres, cut telephone lines, misdirected convoys – in whatever went amiss the hand of the Fifth Column was detected, never the normal workings of muddle or mischance, confusion or plain cowardice.'

In Britain many eyes turned suspiciously to 'foreigners', and especially the waves of refugees who had entered the country since the rise and spread of Nazism. At the beginning of the war 2,000 aliens, suspected German sympathisers, had immediately been rounded up and interned. Now, with Europe in turmoil, the net began to be spread wider; on 10 May, all adult male aliens living in those coastal areas liable to be invasion sites were interned. Six days later, another 7,000 aliens, both men and women, with their children, were interned in the Isle of Man. This did little to calm the press and public outcry so, on the 21st, the government ordered the internment of all other aliens.

The new prime minister was not actually the leader of the Conservative Party; Chamberlain still held that post, and Churchill asked him to continue. Churchill was thus freed to create a coalition government, bringing in such people as Anthony Eden, Kingsley Wood, and Duff Cooper from the Conservatives, Archibald Sinclair, the Liberal Leader, and Clement Attlee, Herbert Morrison and Ernest Bevin from the Labour Party.

On 13 May, Churchill made a speech to the House, setting out the war aims of his new government:

> . . . I would say this to the House as I said to those who have joined this government: I have nothing to offer but blood, toil, tears and sweat. We have before us an ordeal of the most grievous kind. We have before us many, many long months of struggling and suffering. You ask what is our policy; I will say: It is to wage war, by sea, land, and air, with all our might and with all the strength that God can give us, and to wage war against a monstrous tyranny, never surpassed in the dark, lamentable catalogue of human crime. That is our policy.

You ask what is our aim; I can answer in one word: It is victory – victory at all costs – victory in spite of all terrors – victory, however long and hard the road may be; for without victory there is no survival – let that be realised – no survival for the British Empire, no survival for all that the British Empire has stood for, no survival for the urge and impulse of the ages, that mankind should move forward towards its goal.

On the evening of the 14th, the mustering of a citizens' militia, the 'Local Defence Volunteers' or LDV (renamed the Home Guard in July), was announced in a War Office statement, and in a broadcast speech by Anthony Eden. Within a day a quarter of a million men had reported to their local police stations to enrol. Landings by German airborne forces in the Low Countries had produced widespread fears among the British public that hordes of German parachutists, dressed in various disguises (nuns' habits being the favourite) would descend on Britain at any time. Indeed, on the 14th, the BBC broadcast a warning to Germany that captured parachutists dressed in anything other than official German uniform would be shot.

| Chamberlain | Greenwood | Halifax | | Sinclair | Duff Cooper | Alexander | Eden | | K. Wood |
| Churchill | Attlee | | Bevin | | Morrison | | Amery | |

**" ALL BEHIND YOU, WINSTON "**

Cartoon by Low showing how the whole country, in a reflection of the coalition government, was backing Churchill.

On the following day the Dutch Army capitulated. On the 16th a general warning about parachutists was included in the BBC's news bulletin, and next day guards appeared outside the BBC and the various ministries in Whitehall. That day the US Embassy advised all its citizens in Britain to leave as soon as possible via Eire.

Yet the spirits of the British public were still buoyant. On 16 May, a Mass Observation survey summary included, 'People haven't begun to consider that we might actually be beaten. It just hasn't occurred to most people that we can be beaten. The old complacency has been shaken, but it persists. If suddenly shattered, there will be a morale explosion.' There was a distinct split; morale

" Of course, at the moment it's still just a suspicion."

With the fall of the Low Countries, a new myth sprang up. German parachutists were believed to be about to descend (literally) on Britain disguised as, among other things, boy scouts, or nuns, as this Osbert Lancaster cartoon shows.

among the upper and middle classes was very low, probably because they were better informed. On the 18th, for example, Sir Samuel Hoare wrote in his diary, 'Everything finished. The USA no good. We could never get our army out, if we did it would be without any equipment.' On the following day, the civil servant Oliver Harvey noted in his diary, 'Defeatism in London among the richer classes.' The latest Ministry of Information report stated that, among the public at large, morale was still quite good, but the mood was becoming more realistic, 'The morale of women is considerably lower than that of the men.' On the 19th, the Mass Observation summary stated, '. . . today still shows plenty of implicit or unconscious defeatism, and a few open references to German victory.'

Press reporting of the war was still mostly positive; by the 26th, the Allies were reported to be holding the German assault. In fact the French 'War

Committee' was discussing peace talks with Germany. A few days earlier, Churchill had asked the Chiefs of Staff to prepare a report on the worst possibilities. The report, 'British Strategy in a Certain Eventuality', concluded that, should France fall and Italy enter the war, Britain could still hold out if the Navy and RAF continued to control the Channel and the skies above Britain. However, in the longer term, increasing US aid would be necessary for Britain's survival. It should be noted that these conditions related to survival, not victory. That still relied on Germany being unable to keep a war going. Although he knew nothing of the report, King Leopold III of Belgium seems to have independently agreed with its conclusions. That day he told his ministers:

> The cause of the Allies is lost . . . No doubt England will continue the war, not on the Continent, but on the seas and in the colonies, but Belgium can play no part in it. Her role is terminated . . . There is no reason for us to continue the war on the side of the Allies.

That day, the BEF was also preparing to give up the struggle in Europe; Lord Gort, the Commander-in-Chief, abandoned the French plan for a counter-attack, and from that moment all British units headed towards the Channel ports.

What is often called simply 'Dunkirk', that is the withdrawal of the BEF, French and other Allied troops from that town, began on Monday 27 May. That morning, the Germans, having moved up their guns, began to shell the town and ships trying to enter or leave the port. In Cabinet, Churchill spoke of the possibility of a French collapse, and Britain's response to it, 'If the worst came to the worst, it would not be a bad thing for this country to go down fighting for the other countries which had been overcome by the Nazi tyranny.'

On the 28th, according to Mass Observation, public morale was still high, in spite of the announcement of Belgium's surrender, 'There is an unusual lack of real worry as yet today. A strong section still express complete confidence, though in the past few days talk about the inevitability of our victory as a walkover has steadily declined.'

There was another struggle taking place, a secret one which would dictate Britain's response to the fall of France. A struggle of which the vast majority of the British public was unaware, yet its outcome would affect them deeply. It was between those who wished to come to some sort of accommodation with Germany, led by the Foreign Secretary Lord Halifax, and those, led by the Prime Minister, who refused to envisage any such idea.

During May, feelers had been put out by the Italians, still neutral at this point, offering to act as intermediaries in peace talks, just as they had done at Munich. Lord Halifax was keen to follow up their offer, as was the French government, but most of the British War Cabinet believed this was merely a convenient way for the French to pull out of the war in spite of their treaty commitments to Britain.

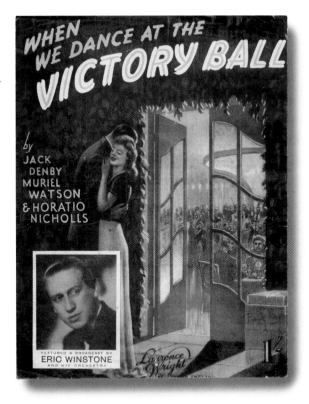

Sheet music: 'When We Dance at the Victory Ball'. Many songs of the period had a wistful air, looking forward to the great times to come when 'it' would all be over.

Matters came to a head at a War Cabinet meeting on Tuesday 28 May. Churchill argued that, if Britain were to start peace negotiations, it would be impossible to pull out. If the government tried to withdraw from negotiations, it would find that the country's resolve had been mortally weakened by the very fact of peace talks, and their implicit prospect of an end to conflict – the country would be deeply split, almost certainly irrevocably so.

In December 1939, Halifax had argued in the cabinet that should the French ever drop out of the war, 'we should not be able to carry on the war by ourselves.' He now argued that Britain would be offered better terms before France fell than after, and that that fall was now certain. Churchill took the opposite view; he believed that, whatever the circumstances, German demands would have to include the neutralisation of the British fleet, and other measures which would emasculate Britain, to prevent Britain from posing any sort of threat to Germany. Even Chamberlain stated that the alternative to continuing the conflict involved a considerable gamble.

Arthur Greenwood, the Minister without Portfolio, acknowledged that either path involved considerable dangers but spoke for many when he said that it did not seem to be the time for capitulation. Churchill went further. With typical pugnacity he said that those countries which went down fighting rose again, whilst those which surrendered tamely were finished.

The meeting adjourned; Churchill then met the entire Cabinet, a meeting at which no-one demurred from his position. Halifax at this point backed down – Churchill, the 'warmonger' of German propaganda, had won – the die was cast, Britain would fight on. Hugh Dalton, who was present, quoted Churchill as saying, 'We shall go on and we shall fight it out, here or elsewhere, and if at last the long story [of the British Empire] is to end, it were better it should end, not through surrender, but only when we are rolling senseless on the ground.'

Thus the 'new' coalition Cabinet represented by Churchill, vanquished the 'old', represented by Halifax, who, in the eyes of many also represented a discredited ideology which had culminated in the shame of Munich, and the disasters of the *Blitzkrieg*. The new cabinet's multi-party make-up had brought in not only new people, but new ideas and ideologies. Socialist concepts of state control and centralisation seemed to be exactly what were needed to put British industry on to a real war footing, and to make other wartime schemes, such as rationing, work effectively.

On 24 August 1939, with war rapidly approaching, the government had rushed through an Emergency Powers Act, which empowered it to make regulations by Orders in Council for the defence of Britain. The Emergency Powers Act had not only brought in a raft of new offences, such as contravening the black-out regulations, it had also been used to give the government sweeping powers. All trade in foodstuffs from abroad was taken over by the Ministry of Food and retail prices of the most important goods were controlled. The state also now had the right to seize just about anything it believed was needed for the war effort: cars, houses, hotels, livestock, farms, and so on. These were a few, a very few, of the dozens of new powers which the government had granted itself. E.S. Turner wrote 'One day sufficed to turn Britain into a totalitarian state.' Many on the right complained of 'creeping socialism', yet many accepted the situation, and the idea of 'war socialism' was born. The *New Statesman* of 1 June pronounced, 'We cannot actually achieve socialism during the war, but we can institute a whole series of Government controls which after the war may be used for socialist ends.'

On 31 May, orders were given for signposts throughout the country to be taken down, milestones to be removed and road names, railway station name boards and so on painted out or removed. There were further measures against foreigners; the BBC announced that, from 3 June, no alien could own any motor vehicle, sea-going craft, aircraft, or even a bicycle without police

**" VERY WELL, ALONE "**

The German *Blitzkrieg* swept across Europe in the summer of 1940, leaving Britain and the Commonwealth standing alone against the Axis forces, but still defiantly fighting, as this cartoon by Low so clearly shows.

permission, and that all aliens would be subject to a curfew. Further, should any alien stay the night away from his or her registered place of residence, it was the duty of the householder where they were staying to report their presence to the local police.

On 4 June, the Dunkirk evacuation came to an end; one third of a million Allied troops, mostly British, had been lifted off. Some saw it as a victory, but many, especially in the military, were only too aware of the pitiful state of the country's defences. The army had left behind in France most of its heavy equipment, guns and tanks, and a great deal of personal equipment and small arms. There was a dire shortage of everything, including men.

George Pringle remembered:

In September 1939 I was ordered to report to a Government medical centre in Renshaw Street, Liverpool. After a brief but thorough examination I was classed as A3. Dunkirk was the first time I began to doubt if Britain would win the war, or even survive. My doubts were further increased when I was reclassified A1 and conscripted into the Army. These were not eased when, wearing khaki battledress, I was given a broom handle to assist in my training to become a killer.

On 5 June, J.B. Priestley began broadcasting a series of talks, called 'Postscripts' on the BBC. These proved immensely popular, though not with the Conservative right, who accused him of being 'leftish'. The reason for this anger was that his talks began to voice a growing sentiment that, post-war, there should be no return to the social conditions of the 1930s. On the 7th the BBC news bulletins reported that the US Embassy 'stressed that this might be the last opportunity for Americans to get home until after the war'.

John Wheatley remembered:

Just after Dunkirk was the lowest time. I remember the father of our evacuee lads came down from Kent about this time for a few days, and how worried he was about the situation; you could feel the anxiety in the air, our backs really did seem to be against the wall. It seemed as if the Germans could have walked in after the fall of France and there was not a lot we could do to stop them. Some people thought that soon the air would be full of human paratroops and Jerry tanks would be rolling through our towns. There was definitely an air of foreboding. We had some other terrible lows, but none as bleak as summer 1940.

On the 10th, Mussolini, not wishing to miss out on the glory or the spoils, brought Italy into the war. His troops engaged the French in the Alps and were soon in trouble; luckily for them, and him, the battle was almost over. This 'act of treachery', as it was seen by many, brought retribution to Italians living in Britain, as the *Cleveland Evening Gazette* of 11 June noted:

> In Middlesborough police acted quickly to round up about 20 Italian aliens in the town. But there were repercussions when a crowd toured the town's streets and virtually wrecked six well-known ice cream establishments in Linthorpe Road, Grange Road, Suffield Street, Newport Road and Corporation Road. Large stones were hurled at plate glass windows and furnished interiors and in some cases interior equipment was used to finish wrecking shop fronts.

When the German forces renewed their advances, the French front on the Somme crumbled before the attack. On 10 June the French government left for Tours and Paris was declared an 'open' city. Four days later German forces entered the capital, while others were advancing far to the south. Winston Churchill flew to Tours to urge the French government to fight on. André Maurois wrote that the Prime Minister was:

> . . . horrified by the complete disorganisation of the country. The airport at which he landed was deserted. No member of the government, no representative, came to meet him. The city was overcrowded with refugees and he had great difficulty in finding the government. There, in a château on the Loire, the French premier told him that he, Reynaud, stood for continuing the struggle but that he might be forced to make way for another government which would ask for an armistice.

Reynaud's plan was to continue the war from French North Africa, but it was defeated in the Council of Ministers by a vote of thirteen to ten. There was now no hope left for France, on the 17th, the 84-year-old Marshal Pétain replaced Reynaud as Prime Minister. Next day the French asked Germany for an armistice.

With France out of the war, few gave Britain much chance, as Winston Churchill recalled in a speech in December 1941, 'When I warned them that Britain would fight on alone whatever they did, the [French] generals told their Prime Minister: "In three weeks England will have her neck wrung like a chicken." Some chicken; some neck.'

Preparations to resist an invasion began in earnest. The ringing of church bells had been banned on the 13th; henceforth they would only be used by the military or the LDV to signal that airborne forces were landing. It was also announced that the August Bank Holiday was to be cancelled. On the 15th the US liner *Washington* sailed from Galway, carrying 2,000 US nationals out of Britain. On the 19th, the British War Cabinet decided that it was not possible to defend the Channel Islands. It was thus decided that the islands be demilitarised, effectively leaving them to the advancing Germans. About one third of the islands' 90,000 inhabitants chose to be evacuated to the mainland.

On the 21st, in the forest of Compiègne, the armistice between France and Germany was signed, to come into effect on the 25th. German newsreels showed Hitler walking jauntily away from the scene, while the soundtrack played the latest German hit, 'Wir fahren gegen England' ('We are marching against England'). Indeed, on the 30th, German occupation of the Channel Islands began and part of the United Kingdom fell under German control.

On 16 July, Hitler issued Directive Number 16 to his armed forces. This began:

As England, in spite of the hopelessness of its military position, has so far found herself unwilling to come to any compromise, I have decided to begin to prepare, and if necessary to carry out, an invasion of England. This operation is dictated by the necessity of eliminating Great Britain as a base from which the war against Germany can be fought, and if necessary the islands will be occupied.

Initial plans envisaged an invasion force of forty divisions – the actual strength of the British Home Forces in August and September was twenty-nine divisions and eight independent brigades, all below, and mostly well below, their official establishment of men and equipment.

On 19 July, Hitler made a speech to the Reichstag, the first part of which

Sheet music. The song title refers to Churchill's famous speech to the Canadian Parliament in which he mocked the pessimistic assessment of the French generals of Britain's chances of survival in 1940: '"In three weeks England will have her neck wrung like a chicken." – Some chicken; some neck.'

was a justification of Germany's claims on Poland, and a condemnation of the war as the work of 'Jewish capitalist war-mongers, their hands stained with blood' and 'Jews and freemasons, armaments manufacturers and war profiteers, international business-men and Stock Exchange jobbers'. Finally, he referred to British promises to fight on:

> I do not know whether these politicians already have a correct idea of what the continuation of this struggle will be like. They do, it is true, declare that they will carry on with the war and that, even if Great Britain should perish, they would carry on from Canada. I can hardly believe that they mean by this that the people of Britain are to go to Canada; presumably only those gentlemen interested in the continuation of their war will go there. The people, I am afraid, will have to remain in Britain. And the people in London will certainly regard the war with other eyes than their so-called leaders in Canada.
>
> In this hour I feel it to be my duty before my own conscience to appeal once more to reason and common sense, in Great Britain as much as elsewhere. I consider myself in a position to make this appeal since I am not the vanquished begging for favours, but the victor speaking in the name of reason. I can see no reason why this war must go on.

It was meant to be an offer of peace, but the following morning's *Times* headline was 'Hitler's Threats to Britain', a line pursued by the rest of the British press. Two days later, in what many saw as the British government's response, Lord Halifax said in a BBC broadcast, 'We shall not stop fighting until freedom is secure.'

On 30 July, Hitler ordered Hermann Göring, head of the Luftwaffe, to prepare 'immediately and with great haste' to commence 'the great battle of the German Air Force against Britain'. Three days later Göring issued his orders to the Luftwaffe.

On the night of 1 August, large numbers of leaflets were dropped by German aircraft over several parts of Britain. These proved to be a record of Hitler's 'Last Appeal to Reason' speech. This was clearly an attempt to go over the heads of the politicians to the people of Britain. Hitler believed that the government was in the hands of warmongers like Churchill who did not represent the people who were still, at heart, the same pacifists who had so welcomed the Munich Agreement. Yet the document was as heavy going as *Mein Kampf*, and virtually the whole speech had been reprinted, perhaps by German Propaganda Ministry personnel too frightened, or too fanatical, to cut any of their Führer's words. Far from rousing the British public to force their leaders to seek peace, the tortuous and rhetorical language meant that it was generally seen as yet more German bombast. Copies were collected up and handed in to police stations, and even auctioned in aid of the Red Cross, but few, very few, took the offer seriously. Hitler's peace feelers were withdrawn and Britain braced itself for the seemingly inevitable.

# INVASION

## NOTICE TO HOUSEHOLDERS

The Government has decided that if the danger of invasion grows everyone who is not needed to man certain essential services may have to leave this town. Plans are being made for the evacuation on threat of invasion of all civilians other than those who will receive a notice on the authority of the Regional Commissioner, requiring them to remain at their posts.

If circumstances permit, the first to be evacuated will be children and their mothers. Arrangements are accordingly being made to enable children and their mothers (or other women undertaking to look after them) to leave in advance of the evacuation of other people. All parents are urged to register their children for this purpose now: children over 14 years who are still attending school may be included. Children cannot be registered unless they will be accompanied by a woman who will be responsible for looking after them. School children whose parents cannot arrange for someone to accompany them when the time comes should be sent away now to join the school parties already in the reception areas—the Council will arrange for this on being requested by the parents.

Children and mothers should register during the period 30th March to 11th April at the nearest school or registration centre shown on the posters which are being exhibited at

[P.T.O.

the schools and elsewhere in the town. At the end of the week the registers will be closed and will not be reopened. No one will be registered who is not in the town when registration starts.

If the Government found it necessary to order the compulsory evacuation of other people after the children and their mothers had gone, conditions might then be very difficult and anyone who can make private arrangements to move beforehand should do so. Free travel vouchers and billeting certificates can be obtained at the Council Offices. If you have in your household any infirm person unable to travel by ordinary train, who desires to be removed, you should if possible, endeavour to make private arrangements for this purpose. But if you are unable to do so you should furnish particulars of the case to the Local Authority: and these will be noted in case it should prove practicable for the Government to evacuate such persons. They could not, however, be moved until after the children and mothers have been evacuated and only limited accommodation in institutions in reception areas is likely to be available.

Ministry of Health.

(18356) Wt. 50077—3955 150m 3/42 D.L. G. 372

A government leaflet advising the public what they should do in the event of an invasion. In the summer of 1940 a great many people believed an invasion was imminent, and quite a few believed Britain would not be able to withstand it.

On 8 August, the Luftwaffe began its large-scale assault on Britain. The first phase comprised attacks on shipping in the Channel and on coastal towns. On the 24th the target became the RAF itself, with attacks on its airfields. Invasion was originally set for mid-August; at the beginning of that month it was postponed until 15 September. By the end of August, at the request of the German Navy, it had been delayed to 21 September. Should invasion not prove possible that month, it would have to be postponed until May 1941.

On 22 August the German long-range guns on and around Cap Gris Nez began their assault on the Dover area (a few ranging shots had been fired over the previous ten days). Two days later the Luftwaffe attacked the RAF sector stations covering London. Some of their planes got lost and London itself was hit, provoking an RAF retaliation against Berlin. This in turn caused Hitler to order a change of tactics to large scale attacks on London.

YOUR COURAGE YOUR CHEERFULNESS YOUR RESOLUTION WILL BRING US VICTORY

A perfect example of propaganda that went wrong. 'Your courage – our victory'. This seemed to many to sum up the 'them and us' society of the 1930s: 'your' sacrifice (for that read the sacrifice of the common people) will bring 'us' (the ruling class) victory!

At this point, with Britain expecting an invasion at any time, the War Cabinet decided to set up a War Aims Committee. Just three months before, Churchill had said in the House that victory was his government's sole aim, yet now a committee was being set up, whose terms of reference included 'to make suggestions in regard to a post-war European and world system', and 'to consider means of perpetuating the national unity achieved in this country during the war'. At first glance it seems incredible; Britain, teetering on the brink of invasion and defeat is considering its post-victory direction. Had the War Cabinet lost touch with reality?

Actually there was method to this supposed madness. Paul Addison wrote, 'Some of those in authority (though not Churchill) believed that it was important for the sake of raising popular morale to announce promises of a better post-war Britain.' It was no coincidence that the War Cabinet was persuaded to do this by the Minister of Information, Duff Cooper, whose department was deeply concerned with public morale – Sir Kenneth Lee, the Director General of the Ministry, had first brought up the idea on 18 June. Yet Churchill had little to do with these post-war ideas. He busied himself with the immediate task of winning the war, while planning social reforms tended to be left to those interested in them, and therefore ideologically suited for them; which usually meant Labour members of the Cabinet.

On 4 September Hitler addressed the faithful at the Berlin Sportpalast.

When people are very curious in Great Britain and ask 'Yes, but why doesn't he come?' We reply: 'Calm yourselves! Calm yourselves! He is coming! He is coming!'

On the 7th, the Luftwaffe turned its sights on the British capital – the Blitz on London had begun. The immediate response of the War Cabinet was to see this as the probable first stage of an invasion, an attempt to cause disruption and confusion. They responded by issuing the codeword 'Cromwell' – placing the country's defences on alert – 'invasion imminent, and probably within 12 hours'. The Army and Home Guard manned their defences and set up road blocks and laid mines. That night, the church bells were rung over a wide area of southern and eastern England and in some places bridges were even blown up. Next day another rumour began: the Germans had indeed launched an invasion but it had been destroyed at sea by the Navy and RAF. Yet all was not over – on the 9th the bells were rung in five Scottish towns.

George Pringle recalled:

After the Battle of Britain our regiment, amongst others, was sent to London. The air raids on London and the suburbs were destroying building after building and killing or maiming hundreds. Our task was to search the bombed buildings for people, alive or dead. Night after night the raids went on; it seemed that nothing was going to stop London from being razed to the ground. I thought this was definitely it and Churchill would ask for a truce.

# CHAPTER 2

# *The Tide Turns*

If the invasion of Britain was to take place on 21 September, an order had to be given on the 11th which would set in motion vital preparations. On that date Hitler postponed any decision until the 14th, and then again until the 17th, on which date his high command learned that he had decided to put it off until the following spring.

On 13 September the British government had announced that it had no intention of leaving London, and it was around this time that public opinion began to change. The Blitz was awful, but survivable; bomb stories began to be the latest thing. Everyone had their own story of a near miss. A *War Weekly* reader in Newcastle wrote, 'A man here has had a good idea, which is helping to swell our local Spitfire Fund. He stands in the street with a notice: "I'll listen to your bomb story for sixpence."'

On Sunday 15 September, the Battle of Britain reached its height. Wave after wave of German aircraft attempted to break through to London, only to meet the RAF. Britain claimed to have shot down 185 enemy aircraft that day and, although the actual total was far lower, the fact that the RAF was still able to put up such stiff resistance disconcerted the Germans, who believed their own propaganda, which boasted that they had all but destroyed the British air force. Soon, daylight raids over Britain would cease; the destruction of the RAF, a key pre-requisite for invasion, had not been achieved. John Wheatley remembered that, 'The public mood became more optimistic by the end of September with the successes of the Battle of Britain, and Winston Churchill was beginning to inspire the nation with his oratory.'

Yet this was only a respite from immediate danger. On 7 October German troops entered Romania, while on the 28th Italy invaded Greece. At home the raids on London and other targets continued, and on the night of 15 November came the devastating attack on Coventry.

On 18 December, Hitler issued the order to begin preparations for invasion – not this time of Britain, but of Russia. The preparations for the attack on his ally would be carried out under the greatest secrecy, which meant that overtly Britain still remained the chief target for both bombing raids and invasion. In fact, Hitler would never again seriously contemplate an invasion of Britain, though no one in Britain knew that. The Germans themselves would not officially discard the idea until February 1942, when those forces earmarked for the invasion were released from the role, while Britain itself did not relax its invasion watch until after the D-Day landings in France in 1944.

In January 1941, Arthur Greenwood was made chairman of the Reconstruction Committee, responsible for planning post-war redevelopment. The morale nature of the post is indicated by the fact that up to February 1942, when he was dismissed, the committee had met only four times. Others were hard at work, however. The economist John Maynard Keynes had been asked by the government to draw up a statement of Britain's war aims. This he completed in January 1941, but his paper was never published. In it he attacked the Versailles Treaty for having ignored economic considerations, and promised that 'the British Government is determined not to make the same mistake again. Mr Bevin said recently that social security must be the first object of our domestic policy after the war.' This determination that Britain's struggle should not be endured in order to go back to the way things had been, reflected much public thinking at the time. Britain was fighting for a better world, or at

Sheet music: 'Till the Lights of London Shine Again'. Another popular song wistfully looking forward to a post-war, post-blackout time.

least a better Britain. The disappointment of the return after the Great War and how the idea of 'homes fit for heroes' had never been achieved and then had disappeared in the grim reality of the Depression, was an enduring theme, which led to much that was still undreamed of in 1941.

After the lull of the winter months, defences against the invasion once more swung into action in early 1941. The following extracts from a letter sent by the Liverpool Victoria Friendly Society to its staff give a fascinating insight into both the continuing expectation of an invasion, and the determination of many, including business, to carry on even if one took place.

To the staff. Re: Invasion.

The Prime Minister in his recent broadcast stressed the fact that the possibility of enemy invasion cannot by any means be dismissed and that even an attempted or partial invasion would doubtless be attended with considerable disturbance of the means of transport and communication, especially in the effected areas . . .

You will readily appreciate that in the case of invasion, military requirements would be supreme, and that, subject to this, the powers of Government departments would be vested locally in the Regional Commissioners, and that apart from compulsory mass evacuation from the five-mile coastal strip, a complete standstill order to civilians is to be anticipated. Obviously, all railways, main and secondary roads would be kept entirely clear for military purposes, and the ordinary means of communication by post, telephone and telegram would be similarly commandeered and would be available, if at all, to the public and business undertakings to a very limited degree . . .

In the case of invasion Collectors should do all they can to keep in active touch with their respective District Managers and Offices, but should the Authorities require them to remove they should, of course, take with them their collecting books, National Health Registers, Stamped Cards and all other important documents, and in the event of losing touch with their own District they should report to the nearest District Manager, Sub-Agent or Branch Office of their Society without delay. If Collectors are unable to hand their cash to the District Office they should bank some to the credit of the Society daily in the District Office Account.

In March the US Lend-Lease Bill was passed. Britain would now find it far easier to get food, and all kinds of vital materials from America. In Greece, too, things were looking good. The Italians were having definite problems, but on 5 April German forces intervened. On 20 April Greece surrendered and the British and Empire forces had to be hastily evacuated.

On 10 May, came one of the war's stranger episodes. Hitler's deputy, Rudolf Hess, crash-landed in Scotland. He claimed he was on a mission to talk to peace-minded individuals in Britain, while the German authorities hinted at madness. That night came the war's worst raid on London. Two waves of bombers attacked between 12.30 and 4.30 a.m. German figures claimed a total of 708 tons of high explosives and 86 tons of incendiaries dropped. Over 1,400 people were killed outright and 1,800 seriously wounded; over 2,000 fires were started, and over 150,000 families were left without water, gas, or electricity.

In *The City That Wouldn't Die*, an account of the raid, Richard Collier records Reg Matthews, a GPO engineer who had worked among the falling bombs since the start of the Blitz, as saying, 'There never was a raid like it, another one like that and they'd have had us on our backs.' And Principal Fire Officer Clement Kerr admitted, 'I shudder to think what would have happened if the Germans had returned.' While Leonard Styles, Southwark's Civil Defence chief, told Admiral Sir Edward Evans, Joint Regional Commissioner for London, 'In my opinion, Sir, two more nights of this and London will be at a standstill.' Luckily they did not return.

Ten days later the Germans struck again, this time at Crete. German paratroopers, so feared in Britain, landed in great numbers, and with great losses on the Island. After a brief but fierce battle, the British forces were evacuated.

On 22 May, the Minister of Health, Malcolm MacDonald, announced the setting up of a committee to look into benefit payments, such as sick pay. Made up of civil servants, the committee was to be chaired by William Beveridge, a well-known economist and Master of University College, Oxford. From this rather unpromising start, the Beveridge Report would eventually emerge. Just one month later, Churchill appointed R.A. Butler President of the Board of Education. Slowly but surely, Butler would steer his education reforms through committees until the Butler Education Act,

The discussion group became part of service life, as troops and, in this case, members of the National Fire Service, debated the direction that post-war society should take.

which created the tri-partite system of Grammar, Technical, and Secondary Modern Schools, and raised the school leaving age to fifteen, was passed in March 1944.

On 24 May, HMS *Hood* was sunk by the *Bismarck*. John Wheatley recalled how devastating the loss was. 'One blow was the sinking of the *Hood*. The Royal Navy must have been shocked by the ease with which the Germans seemed to do it. I remember seeing her with other warships anchored in Torbay a couple of years before the war – she was the pride of the fleet.' It was some consolation that the *Bismarck* itself was sunk on the 27th.

In June 1941, the Army Bureau of Current Affairs (ABCA) was set up. In 1940, the Haining Report had suggested that officers give informal talks and lectures to their men; this had come as a welcome suggestion to many in the Army. Army life at the time was described by one ex-soldier as '90 per cent boredom and 10 per cent sheer bloody terror', and anything to relieve this 90 per cent boredom was recognised as a good thing, especially by the officers who knew from painful experience that boredom could lead to low morale, lack of discipline, and even criminal behaviour.

The director of ABCA was W.E. Williams, from the Workers' Educational Association. He instituted a scheme whereby troops not on active duty would have, at platoon level, a weekly discussion session, on a pre-set topic, led by their officer. Fortnightly bulletins were produced from September 1941 to help the officer with topics. One was called 'War' and covered military events, and another 'Current Affairs'. Much of the latter covered ideas for post-war reconstruction and social policy, and came to be seen by the more traditional Conservatives as hot-beds for radical ideas. This was not helped by the 1943 ABCA handbook which set forth its ideal as creating the citizen soldier who 'must know what he fights for and love what he knows'. Such a quote, from Oliver Cromwell, evoked memories of the Roundhead army of the Civil War – not a view guaranteed to win over Conservative hearts and minds. Churchill was suspicious, but the majority of officers found the scheme useful, and several investigations found little or nothing exceptionable in its workings. What is remarkable was that the scheme was yet another example of how, from early in the war, the question of post-war reconstruction, and the shape that the post-war world would take, was being openly discussed, with official encouragement, at almost every level.

Then on 22 June, German troops invaded Russia. On 12 July an Anglo-Soviet agreement was signed; the British Empire was no longer alone. A country with vast resources in men and materials had become Britain's ally in the struggle against Hitler, and for many this was a great relief. Some, however, could not get over their traditional hatred of Communism. The BBC refused to play the *Internationale* on its 'National Anthems of the Allies' programme, and Churchill fully supported this policy, repeatedly refusing to allow it to be played until at last giving in in January 1942. Yet the increasingly dogged resistance put up by the Russians could not fail to impress even him. The British people began to accept that the vast bulk of Hitler's armed forces was being thrown against this newest ally, and could see that the Russians were withstanding the onslaught. Not only did the Russian people thus soar in British opinion, the general view of the Communist system there, so long portrayed as inefficient, was, by association, also being transformed. Thus the general drift to a more left-leaning view which had begun, first as a reaction to the failures of Chamberlain's Conservative Government, then as an acceptance of 'we're all in it together', and of rationing in terms of 'fair shares for all', was underscored by the gallant struggle of the people of the Soviet Union.

Then, on 7 December, Japanese forces attacked the American Pacific Fleet at Pearl Harbor. The following day Britain and the USA declared war on Japan, and three days later Germany and Italy declared war on the USA. Now Britain had two great powers on its side, and many believed that ultimate victory was assured. But it would take a while for the USA to put itself on a war footing, and for some time all the news in the east would be of defeats and retreats. Hong Kong fell to the Japanese on Christmas Day but the news was held back until after the holiday. There was one piece of relatively good news, however, Josef Goebbels, the German Propaganda Minister, wrote in *Das Reich* newspaper that, while a German invasion of Britain was beset by problems, the same problems applied to an Allied invasion of Europe; it was almost an admission that Germany had given up hope of invading Britain and was digging in for a war of attrition.

In January 1942, to great acclaim, the first US troops to reach Britain arrived in Northern Ireland, but on 15 February came another great blow as the fortress island of Singapore fell to the Japanese.

June 23rd, 1941.

A pair of unlikely socialist comrades greet each other with clenched fist salutes. In June 1941, Germany invaded Russia. Britain had a new ally, and many anti-communist prejudices disappeared overnight, as this cartoon by Osbert Lancaster aptly suggests.

Although the main political parties had declared a truce for the duration, this did not apply to independents, and there were, of course, by-elections from time to time caused by MPs' deaths and other reasons. In March 1942 came the first of a series of government defeats at a by-election, when Mr W.D. Kendall stood as the 'More Production' candidate in Grantham. Mr Kendall was not, however, anti-Churchill, as he said, 'I am not going to pitch into Churchill. I am going to Westminster to give Churchill the help he obviously needs, although he would not tell the electorate so. My job there is the same as my job here [he was the manager of a local engineering firm] – more production.' One month later the government lost two further by-elections to independents, first in Rugby, and then in Wallasey, where George Reakes won after cutting the Conservative vote by a massive 35 per cent.

On 22 June Tobruk fell to the German Afrika Korps, a defeat regarded as a huge disaster at the time. In 1941 it had held out for eight months under siege, to great acclaim; its loss now was a real blow. Four days later Tom Driberg, standing for J.B. Priestley's newly-formed '1941 Committee', took Maldon from the Conservatives. The Committee soon re-emerged as the 'Common Wealth' party, with Priestley as chairman. It was to have some electoral success, defeating Conservative candidates in three by-elections between April 1943 and April 1945, but for most of the independent victors, their success should be seen more as an anti-government, or perhaps even an anti-Conservative vote, as the official Labour and Liberal parties were not contesting the seats.

On 23 October 1942 the Eighth Army began a new offensive. Thus opened the great struggle known at the time as the Battle of Egypt, but which history has simply dubbed El Alamein. After some ten days of hard fighting, the Afrika Korps was broken and sent into full retreat, and on 8 November, in a killer blow to Axis designs on North Africa, US and British forces landed in Algeria and French Morocco, forming a pincer movement against the retreating Axis troops. On 10 November, Winston Churchill spoke about the victory at the Mansion House, using the famous words, 'Now, this is not the end, it is not even the beginning of the end. But it is, perhaps, the end of the beginning.'

But for many in Britain, El Alamein marked the turning point. A real victory at last, and before the Americans had intervened, not an Allied, but a British, or at least a Commonwealth victory. Better still, a victory against the vaunted Afrika Korps, and to top it all, a victory against Rommel, a general that the Allied troops in North Africa had come to regard as a sort of superman. Now Britain could take its place at the victory table with its head held high. Later Churchill was to say, 'Before Alamein we only survived, after Alamein we conquered.'

George Pringle saw these events at first hand:

I was certain we would win the war, when, as part of the First Army, I landed on the beach in North Africa on 9 November 1942. We overcame the French and made our way up to Tunis. Seven months later we trapped over 250,000 German troops between ourselves and the advancing 8th Army.

In December 1942 the Beveridge Report emerged. It proposed sweeping changes to the social security system and the creation of a raft of benefits. The main proposals of the report were the establishment or extension of: disability benefit, industrial disability pensions, unemployment benefit, training benefit, marriage grants, maternity grants, maternity benefit, guardian's benefit, child allowance, retirement pensions, funeral grants and national assistance. The plan also called for the creation of a national medical service, and a department of social security. The course of affairs in post-war Britain was to be radically altered from what had gone before.

In January 1943 US President Roosevelt and Prime Minister Churchill met at Casablanca. It was agreed that only the unconditional surrender of the Axis Powers was acceptable; there would be no deals. As if to underline the change in the Allied fortunes heralded by El Alamein, on 2 February the German Sixth Army surrendered at Stalingrad, followed by the surrender on 13 May of the Axis forces in North Africa. Once again Churchill spoke, 'Ah! But victory is no conclusion; even final victory will only open a new and happier field of valiant endeavour.'

In February the Commons had debated the Beveridge plan, but stiff Conservative opposition had rejected several of its provisions, including the ideas of a national medical service, and a department of social security. From this point on there was a growing suspicion that, for Tories at least, official acceptance of post-war schemes was little more than lip-service for the sake of morale.

On 10 July 1943 the Allied armies landed in Sicily and the long-awaited second front was opened. Just fifteen days later Mussolini was forced from office and on 17 August the last Axis forces were driven out of Sicily. On 3 September the Eighth Army landed on the Italian mainland, and five days later the Italian surrender, secretly signed on the 3rd, was made public. Everything now seemed to be going the Allies' way. On 1 October the Allies occupied Naples, while six days later in their continuing advances the Russians crossed the Dnieper, and on the 13th, the new Italian government declared war on Germany.

Booklets and pamphlets dealing with likely post-war concerns abounded, with titles such as 'How to Obtain Full Employment' and 'Demobilisation and Resettlement'. *Picture Post* ran an article on 'A new idea for industry – the factory discussion group'. The Army Bureau of Current Affairs idea had begun to be taken up by some factories, and the magazine looked at the work of the IBCA (Industrial Bureau of Current Affairs) which was trying 'to co-ordinate factory groups into a national scheme'. The scheme had varying levels of success, depending, of course, on the factory owner's or manager's co-operation.

Conscription into the factories had brought women from all sorts of backgrounds together. In *Millions Like Us* (released 1943), a British flag-waver about women in war factories, the last lines in the film are spoken by the factory foreman to an upper-class conscriptee:

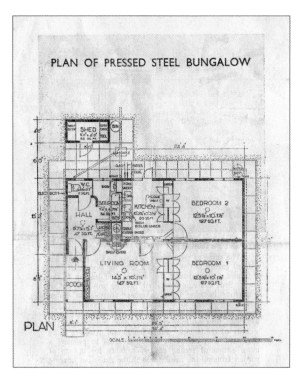

PLAN OF PRESSED STEEL BUNGALOW

PLAN

Plan of a pre-fab from a leaflet issued to servicemen. If they were not exactly 'homes fit for heroes' they were certainly practical homes and as such the pre-fabs proved remarkably popular in the post-war years.

The world's roughly made up of two kinds of people – you're one sort and I'm the other. Oh, we're together now there's a war on, we need to be. What's going to happen when it's over; shall we go on like this or shall we slide back? That's what I want to know.

Radio (or wireless as British people called it then) also played its part. On 20 January 1944 R.A. Butler gave a BBC radio talk on his Education Bill, which was at that time being debated in the House of Commons. In March, the BBC broadcast the first in a series of special programmes on the post-war housing problem, entitled 'Homes for All'.

What could be done to improve the housing situation, especially after the Luftwaffe had done its worst, was a popular concern. In May, the Prime Minister spoke in the Commons about the problems of post-war housing. He told the assembled members that approximately one million houses had been destroyed or damaged by enemy action. 'This offers a magnificent opportunity for rebuilding and replanning, and while we are at it, we had better make a clean sweep of all those areas of which our civilisation should be ashamed.' The first priority would be to repair those buildings which could be put back into use successfully. 'The second attack on the housing problem will be made by what are called the pre-fabricated or emergency houses.' Churchill revealed that there were plans to make up to half a million of these:

Factories are being assigned, the necessary set-up is being made ready, the necessary materials are being earmarked as far as possible, the most convenient sites will be chosen . . . Now, what about these emergency houses? I have seen the full-sized model myself, and steps are being taken to make sure that a good number of housewives have a chance of expressing their views about it.

And not only housewives; by February 1945, plans of pre-fabs, as they became universally known, were being displayed in military camps, both in Britain, and abroad, and suggestion slips circulated to troops. In some places, pre-fabs were even erected in military barracks for the troops to view.

Not everyone was impressed. One wrote to *Picture Post*:

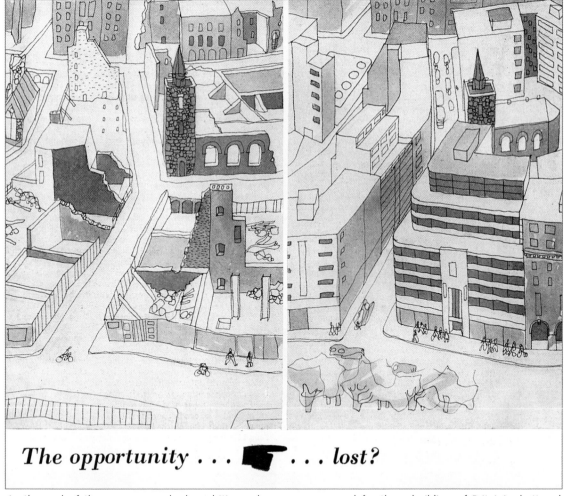

## *The opportunity . . . ◢◤ . . . lost?*

As the end of the war approached, ambitious plans were prepared for the rebuilding of Britain's shattered cities. This illustration is from the County of London Plan.

Would it be impracticable, after the war, to convert the fuselages of the hundreds of thousands of 'planes which will be surplus into at least temporary dwellings? It is a queer reflection that, while we can construct such vast quantities of magnificent aircraft, costing anything from five thousand to fifty thousand pounds each, for our youths to fight and die in, we are compelled, apparently, to construct tin shacks for future generations to be born and live in.

Yet the pre-fabs proved hugely popular, though they would not prove easy to get. Dorothy Richardson remembered:

I had a flat before the pre-fab. I was newly married with a baby, and I was having my second child, so we had two rooms upstairs and the landing. I had a utility sideboard on the landing that I used to wash up on, and we had the front room and the bedroom. I used to pay 10/- [£0.50] a week.

Because we were so cramped I applied for a pre-fab, so I went down to Deptford Town Hall, and I used to go in and see the housing people there. There was a lady – Stanbridge her name was – who was the head of the housing. She used to sit on a platform up on the top there, and she would survey everyone that came in and eventually you got an appointment with her. She said to me, 'How many times have you been down here', and I said 'I come every week', and she said 'And what's been your answer?' so I said 'No'. So she said 'Well, that's your answer now!', I said 'No it isn't'. Then I said 'I shall keep coming until you do something for me', and I went in again and she'd obviously told the people not to help me. I sat there with my two children, and one I was feeding, and I said 'If she won't see me I shall sit here all day', and I did sit there all day, and I fed the baby, and I fed the other child on sandwiches, and I stayed there until, eventually, at four o'clock, she did see me.

So whether that's how I managed to get the pre-fab I don't know, but I was very persistent.

They were lovely. You had a beautiful kitchen – you came into the kitchen from the back door and you had a fridge, then a sink and a boiler, and then you had the gas stove and then cupboards at the end; and that was one complete unit. You had cupboards above, and the other side you had a big cupboard, like a broom cupboard, you could use for storage, and

Throughout Britain, late May and early June 1944 saw troops on the move to their embarkation ports in preparation for the D-Day invasion. These commandos are marching through the outskirts of Southampton shortly before sailing for Normandy. *(Imperial War Museum [IWM] BU1178)*

then there was another cupboard over the other side. We had a kitchen table – it was the first Formica – blue and white check – with stools, which we bought down the Old Kent Road. The living room had a big open fire – that heated the whole place – and there was a lovely big airing cupboard. And all for 6s 7d [£0.33] a week.

Throughout May 1944 the Allied advance continued. On the 9th the Russians captured Sebastopol, and on the 18th the German strongpoint of Cassino, which had held up the advance in Italy for months, at last fell. Then, at midnight on 4 June the BBC news announced the fall of Rome, but

Canadian troops landing on Juno Beach, Normandy, on D-Day, 6 June 1944. *(National Archives of Canada PA-131506)*

even the jubilation aroused by this news was eclipsed when, just two days later the 8.00 a.m. news announced the Allied landings in Normandy. 'Under the command of General Eisenhower, Allied naval forces supported by strong air forces began landing Allied armies this morning on the northern coast of France.' That evening, following the 9.00 news, the first of a new series, 'War Report', was broadcast on the BBC. These were dispatches, recorded on the spot on 'midget' recording equipment (weighing a mere forty pounds!). From the first reports, sent from the Normandy bridgehead, they were a success.

Whether the landings themselves would prove a success was quite another question. At first the battle of Normandy was a hard and bitter slog against determined German opposition, and there was even a possibility in the first few days that the invaders might be forced to withdraw, but gradually the immense superiority of the Allied forces in men and materials began to pay off, though losses on both sides were huge. As the Allies struggled their way out of the 'killing ground' of Normandy, the German Army strove with all its might to avoid being trapped by an Allied pincer movement, leading to vicious fighting as the Germans tried desperately to escape through the ever-narrowing Falaise gap.

At home, however, not all was sweetness and light. Just after midnight on Tuesday 13 June, the German long-range guns in the Pas de Calais area opened up again after what had been a long pause, and shells fell on Folkestone. More than a thousand buildings were damaged by what was Folkestone's heaviest shelling, and they were not alone; eight shells also landed in the borough of Maidstone, twenty-five miles inland.

Just after 4.00 that morning an Observer Corps member noted a 'fighter on fire' in the direction of Boulogne. A few minutes later observers at Dymchurch saw an object spurting red flames and sounding like 'a Model-T Ford going up a hill'. They telephoned the Maidstone Observer Corps Centre: 'Diver, Diver, Diver'. This was the secret code word for Germany's new air-weapon, which Britain had been expecting for over a year, ever since air-reconnaissance had spotted strange goings-on at a place called Peenemünde. Now the first of these new weapons – unmanned aircraft launched from ramps, called by the Germans *Vergeltungswaffe 1* (Reprisal Weapon 1 or V1), was heading north-west over Kent.

Just before 4.15 it suddenly dived to earth and exploded on farmland at Swanscombe. A few minutes later another one exploded at Cuckfield in Sussex, followed soon after by a third which landed on a railway bridge over Grove Road in Bethnal Green. Two houses were destroyed and several others damaged, injuring thirty people and killing six. The V1 assault on Britain had begun. On the 15th the campaign took off in earnest, with over 200 V1s being launched over a period of 24 hours. On the following day the Home Secretary, Herbert Morrison, announced the assault by 'pilotless aircraft' to the House of Commons.

The V1s were launched from specially constructed sites along the French coast between Calais and Houpeville. These, and Peenemünde, were heavily bombed on the 17th, and news of the V-weapon assault gave added impetus to the Allied armies in their push out from Normandy, where, on the 26th, Cherbourg was captured

On 15 August the Allies invaded southern France, and on the following day, Falaise fell to the Allies, as one of the bloodiest battles of the war came to an end. There then followed the breakout of the Allied forces. After the slog of Normandy, the advance became a high speed race, with the Germans in full retreat. The road to Paris, even Berlin, seemed wide open.

The liberation of Paris, 23 August 1944. By then the German retreat seemed to have become almost a rout, and once again people dared to believe that it might be 'all over by Christmas'. *(Crown Copyright)*

Just after noon on 23 August, the BBC reported the liberation of Paris. Robert Reid on the BBC's 'War Report' of 26 August told listeners:

Boulevard cafés began to reopen and to do a thriving trade, and on every street corner hawkers were peddling red, white and blue favours. But even they'd got the Bank Holiday feeling. If you didn't buy a favour they just thrust one in your jacket and wrung your hand if you happened to be British or American. In fact anybody in khaki walking through the streets of Paris to-day moved in a state of perpetual but rather pleasant embarrassment. You were liable any moment to be pounced on, pressed to some matronly bosom, and then passed round the whole family from papa to little René.

The V1 launching sites in France that had escaped the Allied air attacks, now fell to the advancing Allied armies, and the Germans shifted the V1 attack to air-launches from Heinkel aircraft over the North Sea, but these were far less accurate, and far more difficult. From a high in July and August, V1 launchings fell dramatically in September and remained low.

On 3 September, the fifth anniversary of the British declaration of war, British forces crossed the Belgian border and that evening reached Brussels. On the 4th Antwerp fell, and on the 8th Ostend and Liége were liberated. Chester Wilmot described the resulting scenes in the BBC's 'War Report' of 5 September:

Their main trouble was not dealing with the scattered German resistance but getting through the crowds who thronged the roadside every mile from the frontier to Brussels . . . And so it went on until we came to Brussels itself, and there our welcome was wildest of all. There had been Germans in the streets only an hour before, and not a flag in sight; but by the time we arrived every building was plastered with flags and streamers.

With this apparently unstoppable advance the end seemed to be in sight. On the 5th a rumour spread like wildfire that the Germans had surrendered and that the Prime Minister was to announce it to the public that evening. Many listened intently to their wireless that night for an announcement that did not come. Two days later there was an announcement, but only to the effect that the black-out restrictions were being eased, while some Fire Guard and other Civil Defence duties were ending. Duncan Sandys told a press conference that 'except possibly for a few last shots, the Battle of London is over.'

That same day, a new weapon, the V2, was fired on Paris, killing six people in the suburb of Maisons Alfort. At 6.43 p.m. the next day,

8 September, another V2 crashed to earth at Chiswick in West London, killing three and injuring seventeen. People were bewildered, there was no sign of a bomber, and no V1 had been seen or heard; meanwhile the government maintained a wall of silence, blaming this and subsequent blasts on exploding gas mains. The V2, they knew, was a supersonic weapon for which there could be no warning and no defence; how could they tell that to the public? It would not be until 10 November that Churchill would announce the use of rockets against Britain.

On 9 September Luxembourg fell into Allied hands, and two days later elements of the US First Army crossed the German border near Trier; within 100 days of the D-Day landings, Allied troops were on German soil, while on the 15th, US forces were reported to have breached the vaunted German border defences, the Siegfried Line, east of Aachen. Now even the most hardened cynics had no doubt of the Allies' eventual victory, and many began to revive the old saying, or at least the sentiment, 'It'll all be over by Christmas'.

Talk was certainly of peace. The form that the peace celebrations should take was also becoming a major topic of public debate. *Picture Post* magazine, of 16 September, for example, included some interesting letters. One of these favoured planning ahead:

I believe many people wish to avoid the scenes that were enacted last Armistice Day [1918]. Presumably, without warning, we shall be subject to the same unbridled surge of emotion on the declaration of peace. I suggest that a definite programme of celebration might be prepared and published before the great day.

Another reader suggested:

I wish to express my feelings of horror that a paper of your standing should give publicity to Zoe Gail's dangerous verses, which advocate that on the day the war ceases – when our hearts should be filled with gratitude to God, and to the men and women who have died to deliver the world from tyranny – 'England this day expects the nation to be tight'. Such an England would be totally unworthy!

There were even ideas for bringing peace closer:

**FARE PROSPECTS** — *by Illingworth.*

Taxi driver Lord Woolton, the Minister for Reconstruction, prepares to steer John Citizen through the post-war fog into an uncertain future.

Permit me, through your columns, to congratulate the President of the Board of Trade upon discovering the perfect secret weapon. I refer, of course, to his Utility safety razor blades. Having used one with devastating effects, I can vouch for their general efficacy. I suggest that Mr Dalton should forthwith have all his surplus stock dropped on the enemy. I feel sure it would hasten the ending.

The Beveridge Report was not going to go away, as Barbara Wootton, chair of the Social Security League, wrote:

The Social Security League was founded to prevent the Beveridge Plan from becoming one of those noble, lost causes whose ghosts haunt the vaults of British History. As a principle, social security has the assent of all political parties; it has seized popular imagination and is the topic of countless discussion groups, within the Forces and among civilians. But there are powerful interests at work to undermine the Beveridge Plan, relying on the shortness of public memory and the Treasury's tendency to find, when the time comes, that the requisite money is not available.

The Allied armies moved relentlessly on. On the 17th members of the Allied airborne divisions landed in Holland; two days later Finland signed an armistice, and on the 22nd, the Canadians captured Boulogne, followed by Calais on the 30th. On 4 October Allied troops landed in Greece. On the 13th it was the turn of Athens to be liberated and on the 21st Belgrade.

And of course, all the while, the British and US air forces were wreaking terrible revenge on Germany's towns and cities in 1,000-plus bomber raids. On 14 October, four and a half thousand tons of bombs fell on Duisburg in just twenty-five minutes. A fortnight later it was Cologne's turn. 'From one end of the city to the other, you can count the buildings that have not been shattered on your fingers', Richard Dimbleby reported. By then, however, the Allied airborne operations in Holland had not achieved all their objectives and the swift rush of the other Allied forces had slowed considerably as the Germans regrouped.

By the end of November the Allied advance had been all but brought to a halt. The German forces had fallen back on a defensive line comprising the concrete emplacements of the Siegfried Line, backed up by flooded rivers. Allied forces prepared for a grim defensive action by the Germans, but this was not their plan. Their strategic reserve, the Sixth Panzer Army, had been re-equipped, and placed under the command of Field Marshal Gerd von Rundstedt – he had planned and directed the German breakthrough in the Ardennes in 1940, and was now hoping for a re-run of that action.

Nine days before Christmas he launched his counter-attack; twenty divisions had been put at his disposal, including just about every German armoured division available in the west, and one thousand aircraft. Once again, he would strike through the Ardennes, only this time his target was not northern France, but to cross the River Meuse to take Liège, and if possible Antwerp. The whole plan depended on surprise and speed. In the event the attack achieved all this and more, and his troops pressed on with a savage determination, punching through the US First Army lines in several places.

Allied air superiority was useless when poor weather meant that aircraft were grounded. Once through the American line the attackers pushed on, encountering little in the way of organised defence from the shocked and untried American troops behind the front line, who had, like so many of their leaders, been caught completely unawares. This surprise was compounded by English-speaking German commandos from the Brandenburg Brigade, led by Colonel Otto Skorzeny, who had been infiltrated behind the lines in American uniforms. They set about adding to the confusion among the defenders, altering signposts, attacking dispatch riders and isolated troops; even their imagined presence caused disarray as trigger-happy Allied units opened fire on each other. The Allies rapidly fell back, and many newly liberated towns and villages were abandoned to the advancing German forces, to the stunned disbelief of their citizens.

Yet not all the American defenders had given way. The German assault had been held in several places by dogged defenders, notably by US airborne troops in Bastogne, and the defensive line along the Meuse held. By the 23rd, weather conditions had improved, and Allied aircraft were able to take to the skies, harrying the Germans and dropping supplies to the besieged defenders. German reinforcements failed to arrive in any numbers and their forward units near the Meuse were cut off and destroyed. On the 27th US troops finally re-established contact with the defenders of Bastogne.

In this, the final week of 1944, the German assault began to peter out, and by the first week of the new year American forces, now reinforced by units of the British Second Army, began to push the attackers back to their starting point. On 1 January, an intense air battle took place, with the Luftwaffe losing 160 fighters in less than two hours. By the middle of January the situation was well under control, and by the end of the month the Allies were once more advancing into new ground.

It had been six weeks of savage fighting; the German Army had made its first, and last, major counter-attack since D-Day. Remorselessly pushed back, like a cornered beast it had turned and attacked in a last desperate bid to reverse the course of the war. That bid had failed; there would not be another. Had they managed to reach Antwerp they might, just might, have caused another general Allied retreat such as that of 1940, although this is most doubtful. Yet, slim as the chance was, it had been their last. It had been expensive; they had lost irreplaceable men, tanks, and aircraft. All they could now do was to slow down the inevitable Allied spring offensive.

WHEN THE BELLS PEAL OUT ONCE MORE

Did you hear the Bells
break silence
on that great November morn?
Did you feel the thrill of Victory?
Did they tell of Hope reborn
for the early termination
of the strife and stress of War?
And our Loved Ones safe returning
When the Bells Peal Out
Once More?
NOVEMBER 15th 1942

'When the Bells Peal Out Once More'. Many people looked forward to the end of the war and a return of the little, ordinary things, such as the church bells, silent since June 1940.

In Britain, on 3 December, in a sign that a German invasion was no longer a possibility, the Home Guard was stood down. In the east, the Russians were also advancing; by 6 February they had crossed the Oder, a mere thirty-three miles from Berlin. The following day Churchill met Roosevelt and Stalin at Yalta, where the fate of post-war Germany was decided; it was to be split up into zones occupied by Russia, the USA, France, and Britain. On the 13th Budapest fell to the Red Army, while on the 22nd, 6,000 Allied planes bombed the Reich. That same day, the Turkish National Assembly voted unanimously to declare war on Germany and Japan as of 1 March.

By February the Allies had regrouped their forces and renewed their push through the Reichswald and across the Roer. Starting slowly, by March their advance was once again rapid. On 1 March, Mönchengladbach fell, and on the 2nd the German Army retreated across the Rhine. Cologne was entered by US troops on the 5th, and two days later units of the US First Army seized the Ludendorff Bridge over the Rhine at Remagen intact.

As the Allies moved into Germany, more and more prisoner of war camps were liberated. Leslie Kerridge had been captured just forward of the El Alamein line in July 1942. By 1945 he was a prisoner in Stalag IVB near a village called Mühlberg-on-Elbe, about twenty-five miles from Leipzig. Like many POWs at this time he was looking forward to liberation, yet with a feeling of trepidation:

All the Germans we saw wore very long faces as they knew very well what would happen to them if the Russians arrived before the British or Americans. It certainly began to look as if the Russians would be the first to arrive at the Elbe. We were not very pleased to see the defence preparations they were making because it looked as if the Germans intended to make a stand, a state of affairs which would have very much placed us in the battlefield. Taking all into consideration neither the Germans or us had very much to be overjoyed about, as they were liable to be overrun and we did not enjoy the prospect of being exposed to fire from both sides with no possible hope of finding any sort of protective cover.

It was decided that a good idea would be to mark the camp with large letters showing that it was a POW camp. The Germans showed amazing enthusiasm for this scheme, their motive being not hard to guess. Accordingly the rugby pitch was chosen as the site, and large seventy-foot-long letters placed on it composed of large stones painted with whitewash. 'POW' was also marked on the roofs of the huts in each corner of the camp.

The approaching end did not signal any diminution of the V1 and V2 attacks. In fact February and early March 1945 marked an increase in the assault, with about a hundred V2s falling in south-east London during March. On 8 March, one fell on London's Smithfield Market killing 110 people and injuring 123.

At 4.57 p.m. on Monday 27 March the last V2 to land on England fell in the back gardens between Court Road and Kynaston Road in Orpington. Fifty-six residents were wounded, and Mrs Ivy Millichamp, aged thirty-four, of No. 88 Kynaston Road, became the last civilian in Britain to be killed by enemy action (although several more would die of wounds already received). Overall 1,115 rockets had fallen on Britain.

The following morning the final 'incident' of the air attack on Britain took place just two and a half miles away, when a V1 landed at Scadbury Hall, in Chislehurst. Of course, no-one at the time realised that these were to be the last; there was never a formal announcement that the campaign was over, and residents in the target areas could not really breathe easily until the announcement of peace.

As the end approached, a new feeling was abroad. *Westminster at War* describes it:

During the last months, a new neurosis flourished, the anxiety against being killed by 'the last bullet'. Many who had survived the years of danger felt the flutter of their hearts in their mouths when they imagined the last unlucky chance. When people heard of the final shelling of the luckless Dover, when they heard on some fine days the resonance of our guns liquidating the last German garrisons in the besieged French Channel ports, or when the boom of a rocket suddenly erupted in the London air – many felt anxious and irritated at what seemed a futile killing when the main course of the war was so patently decided.

On 29 March British troops entered Münster, while the Russians captured Danzig. They were also approaching Stalag IVB, as Leslie Kerridge remembered:

We knew now that our release was well on the way and were hoping that it would be achieved by the Americans and not the Russians. One day the German Commandant called the Camp Leader to his office and asked whether we would like to be moved across the river so as to be released by the Americans. His idea was very clear to us all but as we had received the radio message sent by General Montgomery that all POWs and slave workers were to stay put, we refused. The Poles, however, decided to make this trip as they were obviously not very keen on being released by the Russians.

We had long been expecting to be evacuated from the camp to be taken deeper into German occupied territory, but we had never expected to be asked whether we would like to move out or not. We had all been prepared for such a move for a long time and had all the necessities packed

Something to look forward to!

**Mackintosh's**
"always in quality street"

TOFFEES AND CHOCOLATES

An advert that appealed on two levels. One could look forward, not only to a time when sweets would not be rationed, but also when the black-out would be gone and the sight of a lit-up shop window would not bring the call of 'Put that light out!'

ready. Some fellows had even made small hand-carts from odd pieces of wood and bed boards. We were very lucky to stay where we were as everyone had now heard of the long and arduous marches forced upon some POWs. As things were now, all our latest discomforts were being forgotten in the excitement of our impending release. One night very late we began to hear guns firing in the distance and all made up our minds that we were in for it in a big way.

We were all excited at the prospect of very soon being free once again and we were also very worried at the thought of being involved in a pitched battle. We just did not know what to think. All day long fellows could be seen peering into the distance watching for any sign of a liberating force.

On 15 April British troops entered the concentration camp at Belsen and found around 35,000 corpses. On 16 April, the British 7th Armoured Division captured Stalag XIB near Fallingbostel, which held 6,500 British and US troops, including 700 captured at Arnhem. Liberation was close for Leslie Kerridge, too:

[On 22 April] the Camp Leader was once again summoned to the office of the German Commandant and told to make ready to take over the camp as in all probability we would find that the Germans had evacuated by next morning. The Camp Leader had apparently foreseen this occurrence and

*To all those good things*

*which victory*

*will bring back*

# Schweppes

Schweppes advert from early 1945. The end of the war held the promise of the return of a great many products which had disappeared as the war went on. Sadly it would be many years before some things became generally available again.

had plans already made to deal with it. A guard was detailed that night and was warned to stand by ready to be called out at any time. Great excitement prevailed in the camp when this news was announced. One of my pals was detailed for the guard and at three o'clock in the morning he was called from his bed. The Germans had left the camp and a British guard was posted in all the sentry boxes and on the gate.

The next morning, St George's Day, we were all up very early. Not a sound of warfare could be heard and we began to wonder if we had been by-passed by the Russians. Roll call was held as usual, after which we went back into the huts to partake of one of the very frugal breakfasts we had been having for several weeks. It must have been about half an hour after roll call that the cry went up in the road outside that 'they' had arrived. We did not believe it at first, it just seemed that it could not be true until we all went into the road and saw a huge crowd at the main gateway surging around four horsemen who turned out to be Russian Cossacks. They were very stern faced and business-like young men armed, not with the traditional sabre of the Cossack, but very modern automatic weapons. They were quite unaffected by the tumult which they caused but merely delivered a message from the Russian general, which said, 'You are free. Go out of the camp, loot and do anything you wish.'

The excitement which we had always expected when our liberators arrived turned out to be an awful flop. Instead we all experienced a feeling of intense relief when long pent-up emotions almost broke loose. Many of us had to grit our teeth hard to hold back tears of sheer joy which welled into our eyes. It was all very different from what we had expected. After we had recovered from the first shock of being free men again we all went back into the huts which were humming like a lot of bee hives.

On 24 April, Heinrich Himmler, head of the Nazi SS, met with Count Bernadotte, President of the Swedish Red Cross. Himmler offered unconditional surrender to the USA and Britain, but not the USSR, thus attempting to fulfil the Nazis' dream of splitting the Allies, and at the same time enabling the German forces to concentrate on the Soviet armies. The Allies, however, refused to take the bait, responding that surrender would only be acceptable if offered to all the Allies.

On the 25th, as if to underline this unity, elements of the US First Army met up with forward Russian units at Torgau, amid a blaze of publicity. Edward Ward reported that:

I saw soldiers of the First American and the Red Armies throw their arms round each other's necks and kiss each other on the cheeks. I even had to undergo this greeting myself from a burly Ukrainian soldier . . . A Russian lieutenant sat on a wall playing an accordion and singing Russian songs, and the doughboys joined in. Drinks were passed round and everyone was happy.

That same day Berlin was surrounded.

One month after the last V2 fell, there was still worry about their reappearance. On the 26th, Churchill was asked in the Commons 'whether he was now able to make a statement about the rocket attacks?' 'Yes, they have ceased', he replied. Not to be put off, his interrogator, Mr Hutchison, pressed him, 'Is there any prospect that they are likely to be resumed?' The Prime Minister replied, 'Well, it is my duty to record facts rather than indulge in prophecy, but I have recorded certain facts with a very considerable air of optimism, which I trust will not be brought into mockery by events.' No doubt he had in mind Duncan Sandys' somewhat premature announcement the previous September that, 'Except possibly for a few last shots, the Battle of London is over.'

In the same session of parliament the question of suitable victory celebrations had arisen. Sir Percy Hurd said that, 'It would be madness for us to be ringing joy bells and feasting while fighting was still going on elsewhere.' Churchill agreed in part, 'I think great caution should be observed in any celebrations. However, great events may occur which, even if they do not affect any particular locality, would stir the people here, and they might indulge in some few moments of rejoicing before returning to their heavy task.' Lady Astor then asked, 'Is that not all the more reason why we should keep strictly sober?' to which Churchill's response was, 'We will trust to the noble lady to set us an example in this.' The following day, the *Daily Express* stated that, 'Today's favourite American guess on VE-Day [is] 6 June.'

On 28 April Mussolini was captured by Italian partisans at Dongo, Lake Como, while attempting to escape to Switzerland dressed as a German soldier. With him were his 25-year-old mistress, Clara Petacci, and several members of his 'Republican Fascist' government. The entire group was summarily executed by partisans in the nearby village of Giuliano di Mezzegere. After the BBC reported Himmler's offer of surrender in a news bulletin, Hitler went into one of his worst rages, ranting about the treachery of the man he had dubbed 'Faithful Heinrich', and declaring that 'the war is lost'. Subsequently he dictated his 'political testament', naming Grand Admiral Dönitz as his successor.

On the 29th the bodies of Mussolini and his party were taken by lorry to Milan, where Republican Fascists, refusing to believe the reports of his death, continued to fight in the streets. To convince them that Il Duce was really dead, the Committee of Liberation decided to display the bodies of Mussolini and Petacci in public, and so they were hung up by their feet in front of a garage in the Piazza Loreto. Such a gruesome end underlined Hitler's conviction that he must not be taken, dead or alive.

That same day the German South-Western Command, which included all German and Italian Fascist forces in Italy and the southern provinces of Austria, numbering over one million men, surrendered to Field Marshal Alexander at Caserta. The surrender was to take effect from 2 May, and news of it was not released until that date. In Berlin, with the Reichs Chancellery under steady Russian fire, Hitler married Eva Braun.

# CHAPTER 3

# *The End Is Nigh*

Croydon shared the general excitement during the first week in May.
"Peace' might break out at any time," as the phrase went. The churches
displayed notices that there would be services of thanksgiving
immediately on its declaration. The town prepared to celebrate.
*Croydon and the Second World War.*

Surveys were carried out asking, 'How will you spend V-Day?' Eighteen per
cent answered that they would be 'going wild', or 'dancing in the street'.
The government, however, had other views. All-in-all, the authorities
thought it should be a more sober, dignified affair. Newspapers also carried
articles in which the great and good talked about victory and what they
would be doing on V-Day. Lord Vansittart said, 'How shall I spend it? I shall
enjoy it at home, quietly and soberly, though I shall certainly visit my cellar
and prepare for the best. But I shall also visit the everlasting hills visible
even in the mild undulations of Buckinghamshire.'

Robert Lynd told readers that, 'I prefer to celebrate peace by remaining
peaceful.' Like many others, he had long ago made himself a promise:

I will change my waistcoat. In the week in which the war began I made a
foolish vow, not realising that the war would last so long. Hitler . . .
declared that he would wear the same coat that he was then wearing until
he had won the war. To counter this vow . . . I decided that I would wear
the same suit that I was wearing till Hitler was beaten.

First, however, the seat of the trousers gave way beyond possibility of
patching, so I was left with only the jacket and waistcoat to represent the
suit. Then the jacket disappeared at the elbows and developed rips in the
cloth and gashes in the lining to such a degree that I was left with the
waistcoat alone to enable me to preserve my vow. And lately, the waistcoat
has been, so to speak, on its last legs . . . So afraid have I been lest any of

my enemies – or even of my friends – should see it in recent years that I have worn a pullover to conceal it even when the thermometer was registering a heat wave that threatened me with apoplexy . . . And now I shall be able to discard it and put on a waistcoat that I have not worn for nearly six years. Probably on V-Day I will light a bonfire in the garden and spend the rest of the day waistcoat burning.

## TUESDAY 1 MAY

British and US bridgeheads across the Lower Elbe linked up, while General Patton's Third US Army reach the Czech border north-east of Passau. Tanks of the Third Army reached Branau-am-Inn, Hitler's birthplace. The German forces in Denmark were reported to be 'evacuating the country with all speed', while in Italy, Marshal Graziani, and the German chief of staff in Italy, Lieutenant-General Pemsel, announced the surrender of the Italian Fascist Ligurian Army and ordered all troops to lay down their arms.

At 9 p.m. that night the German radio stations at Bremen and Hamburg played the Wagner Tannhäuser Overture and a piano concerto by Weber. These were repeatedly interrupted by the words 'Please stand by for an important announcement!' After about half an hour the music finished and the radio went silent for a while. Then, at 9.40, the announcer returned: 'Achtung! Achtung! The German Broadcasting System is going to give an important German government announcement for the German people.' This was followed by Wagner's Rheingold, and the slow movement from Brückner's Seventh Symphony. Finally, at 10.25 there came the awaited message: 'It is reported from the Führer's headquarters that our Führer, Adolf Hitler, has fallen this afternoon in his command post in the Reich Chancellery fighting to his last breath against Bolshevism.'

The radio went on to name Grand Admiral Dönitz as the new Führer; Dönitz then spoke:

The Führer has fallen. He fell faithful to his great ideal to save the peoples of Europe from Bolshevism. He staked his life and died the death of a hero. With his passing one of the greatest heroes of German history has passed away. In great reverence and sorrow we lower our flag before him.

German soldiers and civilians waiting to be taken into custody. The overriding fear was of falling into the hands of the vengeful Russians, and both German troops and civilians were desperate to surrender to the Western Allies. *(IWM BU5729)*

Dönitz then stated his 'determination to continue the struggle against Bolshevism', and ended by urging the armed forces to fight on:

> The oath of allegiance you swore to the Führer now applies to each one of you without further formality to myself. German soldiers; do your duty. The life of our people is at stake.

Throughout the broadcast, a 'ghost voice' continually cut in, urging Germans to strike, and telling them that the struggle was not worthwhile. Ursula von Kardoff, a German journalist who knew most of the plotters who had tried to kill Hitler in July 1944 and was sympathetic to their views, kept a diary throughout the war. Her entry for this date includes:

> Hitler is dead. Bärchen, Bürklin and I have just heard it on the radio – Bürklin's driver has gone. Hitler's successor is Dönitz. He made a rather

feeble speech. . . . So this is the moment which I have so ardently desired for years past, for which I have tearfully prayed. What happens now?

In Britain, the Home Office sent a letter to local authorities setting out the plans for victory celebrations. 'News that the war is over will be given by the Prime Minister in a special B.B.C. broadcast. This may be given by Mr Churchill at any hour of the day or night in the very near future.'

This would be followed by a broadcast to the Empire by the King at nine o'clock in the evening. The letter suggested that churches and chapels be opened on VE-Day 'for private prayer', and their bells be rung. VE-Day, and the day following, would be public holidays. The Sunday following would be a national day of prayer and thanksgiving, accompanied by local parades in which representatives of the armed and civil forces would take part; special services were to be held in London, which the King would attend, and in Belfast, Edinburgh and Cardiff, where he would be represented. The government circular continued:

> There will be no objection to bonfires, but the Government trusts that the paramount necessity of ensuring that only material with no salvage value is used, and the desirability of proper arrangements with the National Fire Service or [fire] guard against any possible spread of fire, will be borne in mind. In neighbourhoods where this is likely to arise, the danger of forest fires should also be kept prominently in view.

All public buildings in London, including Buckingham Palace and the Houses of Parliament would be floodlit. Street lighting would not, however, be fully restored, 'because of the fuel and labour shortage', and the dim-out would be continued in coastal areas. The government reported that the coastal black-out needed to be maintained until it was clear that all U-boats had received instructions to cease hostilities and were known to be complying with them. Obviously they had in mind the devastation that the German submarine wolf-packs had been able to inflict on shipping along the US coast after America's entry into the war. The black-out had been very poor, and ships silhouetted against the bright lights from the shore had proved easy pickings. However, on VE night and the following night, authorities inland could use any floodlighting facilities they had, and in addition, the armed forces were to make available any lighting devices that could be spared, including searchlights.

The government was anxious that a wide range of local facilities should be available to the public, including indoor entertainment, and the letter suggested that theatres, cinemas, and music-halls should be encouraged to remain open, and further recommended that, in the case of public-houses and dance halls, 'Applications by licensees for special orders of exemption or extension of drinking hours on the evening of VE-Day should be considered sympathetically.' However, 'No exemption should be granted in respect of the afternoon break' nor 'on the day following VE-Day'. Further, 'They would not suggest that theatres, music-halls, and cinemas should remain open later than the hours prevailing before VE-Day.'

In spite of VE-Day and the day following being declared public holidays, the government 'hoped' that businesses selling and distributing food would remain

Adverts reminded the British public, if they needed any reminding, of the joys of demobilisation to come.

After the vicious fighting in Normandy pictures of large numbers of German troops surrendering became ever more common as more and more German personnel realised that the Allied victory was now inevitable. (*Crown Copyright*)

open for a few hours. The Ministry of Food suggested that grocers ought to remain open for one hour, maybe two, as should tobacconists and post offices, and that dairymen would deliver milk on both days. They further suggested that bakers should continue to make bread after the Prime Minister's announcement of victory, to produce sufficient bread but, 'Although it is expected that the public will be able to obtain bread supplies during the V Holiday housewives are advised to carry in their homes slightly more bread than usual.' Fishmongers and butchers 'and other purveyors of perishable food' should stay open 'long enough to avoid waste', while 'restaurants and cafes are expected to be open on both VE days.' This introduces two terms which we would find unusual: 'the V Holiday', and the two 'VE days'.

The National Union of Retail Tobacconists recommended that shops should be kept open for three hours after the victory announcement; although this might be a somewhat pointless exercise. In an unrelated article, that day's *Daily Mail* pointed out that:

> The cigarette shortage is as acute now as it was before the budget, when smokers, unable to get regular supplies of popular brands, blamed shopkeepers for withholding stocks in anticipation of increased duty.

The *News Chronicle* commented:

> Finding nothing better to do in these last momentous weeks, some Home Office bureaucrats have prepared a circular on how you are to behave on V-Day.
>
> They tell you that the churches will be open for services and private prayer and that, if you are really careful about salvage and don't live too near the sea, you can light a bonfire.
>
> You don't have to be an archbishop, a dustman, or a schoolboy to feel that this circular is a piece of impertinence. Our troops in Germany would be shocked to think that we were not going to celebrate V-Day in a manner worthy of a free people – in other words, exactly as we decide ourselves.

Sybil Morley recalled:

> Strange to say, at home the war had been announced over (by the Americans at their camp over their familiar Tannoy system) a week before it was officially announced in Britain! My father and sister carried out our plan of putting all the lights on in the house minus black-outs! Only to discover it was a false alarm! Fortunately the Americans had realised their mistake and so it only happened for one evening.

## WEDNESDAY 2 MAY

The British newspapers reported Hitler's death. The *Daily Mail* commented that, 'The probability is that he was mad and that his own henchmen murdered him rather than allow him to fall into Russian hands and allow the world to learn the truth.' In the still-occupied Channel Islands the flags flew at half mast.

At 3 p.m., Berlin surrendered to the encircling Soviet armies. German troops in Italy accepted unconditional surrender, and one million men were taken prisoner. In Norway, negotiations were reported to be going on for the surrender of the German garrisons there, while German troops were leaving Denmark 'with all speed'.

Official plans for the approaching VE-Day were announced in the newspapers. Details were given of Churchill's speech, which 'may precede or follow a statement in the House of Commons', and would give details of the surrender terms. The papers spoke of the surrender, pointing out that the Allies would require representatives of the German High Command to sign it so that, 'Future generations of Germans will not be able to claim a second time that the politicians . . . stabbed the soldiers in the back.'

Just when VE-Day would be was a matter of general speculation. The previous day, Churchill, speaking in the House, had promised that if 'information of importance' on the end of the war, reached the government, while parliament was sitting 'as it might do', he would intervene to make an announcement. The *Daily Mail* commented:

> He gave every indication that events were marching to a climax which might be reached at any moment. The general impression last night was that VE-Day is not far away. It may be to-day (not a few people in high places were confident that it would be to-day), or possibly to-morrow.

In Europe, German General Blumentritt sent an emissary to his British opponents, who were told that General Blumentritt commanded all the German forces between the Baltic and the Weser River, and desired to surrender his army group. A rendezvous was agreed, and a meeting scheduled for that Friday. Meanwhile, outside Hamburg, a German colonel and his staff crossed the British lines, guided by a captured British naval officer, with a letter from Field Marshal Busch, commander of the area, requesting surrender negotiations.

That day the Chiefs of Staff received a report from the Joint Intelligence Sub-Committee that there was no longer any risk of flying bomb attack, and only a very slight chance of a rocket attack, subsequently it was decided to discontinue all counter-measures; over a million civil defence workers would receive four weeks notice starting on 2 June, and the Royal Observer Corps was also to be stood down. All anti-gas precautions were relaxed, the orders for the provision and maintenance of public shelters were discontinued, and all restrictions on lighting, except in some coastal areas, were removed.

## THURSDAY 3 MAY

In neutral Portugal, Hitler's death was announced, and official flags were flown at half-mast for the next twenty-four hours. In neighbouring and officially neutral Spain, a requiem mass would be sung for Hitler on 12 May, to which Falangists turned up in force. Just the previous day, Pierre Laval, chief of France's collaborationist government, had fled to Spain accompanied by his wife and four of his ministers, seeking sanctuary. He was asked to leave, but refused to do so and was interned.

General Wolz, the German garrison commander of Hamburg, Germany's second city, met the British commander outside the city, and, the surrender successfully negotiated, the two rode into Hamburg at the head of the British forces.

The whole German defence system in north-west Germany had effectively collapsed, with Hamburg occupied, and Kiel declared an open city, while British and Russian troops linked up near Wismar. The BBC reported:

> The general surrender of the German forces opposing the Second British Army may now come at any hour; except in the pocket west of Bremen there is no longer any real opposition on General Dempsey's front, and pilots today reported that there are white flags flying from houses fifty miles behind the nominal enemy lines.

Four high-ranking German officers bearing the white flag drove into the British lines. The party was headed by Admiral von Friedeburg, who had

taken over from Admiral Dönitz as the Commander-in-Chief of the German
Navy when Dönitz became the new Führer. With von Friedeburg was
General Kienzl, chief of staff to Field Marshal Busch, commander of the
northern German army group, and their aides.

The four German emissaries were taken to Montgomery's field HQ at
Luneberg Heath, where the field marshal asked them what they wanted.
They replied that they wished him to accept the surrender of the three
German armies which were withdrawing before the Russians in the
Mecklenburg area. Montgomery replied:

> No, certainly not. These German armies are fighting the Russians.
> Therefore if you surrender to anyone it must be to the forces of the Soviet
> Union. It has nothing to do with me. I have nothing to do with the
> happenings on my eastern flank. It is the business of the Russians; it is the
> Russian front. You go and surrender to the Russian commanders. The
> subject is closed.

The *News Chronicle* of Saturday 5 May reported how the negotiations
continued:

> Then the German commanders proposed a complicated and diverse
> military programme covering the next few weeks, in which the British
> Second Army would advance slowly while at the same time the Germans
> would retreat slowly.

Montgomery replied, 'No, I will not discuss what I propose to do in the
future.'

Speaking to reporters, Montgomery described what happened next. He
said to the Germans:

> 'I wonder whether you officers know what is the battle situation on the
> Western Front? In case you don't, I will show it to you.' I produced a map
> which showed the battle situation.

This was the final straw. Demanding the unconditional surrender of all
German forces in the north, he told them that, should they refuse to do so,
'then I will go on with the war, and will be delighted to do so. All your
soldiers and civilians may be killed.'

The four German officers replied that they had no authority to agree to these demands. It was decided that von Friedeburg and his aide Major Friede would go back through the German lines to consult their superiors, which they did between 3.30 and 4.00 p.m.

The three representatives of the German armed forces, led by Admiral von Friedeburg (*second from left*), Admiral Wagner (*third from left*), and Major Friede (*right*), arrive to see Field Marshal Montgomery. *(IWM BU5737)*

## FRIDAY 4 MAY

The two German officers returned to Monty's HQ at about 5.00 p.m. with complete acceptance of the unconditional surrender terms.

At 6.10 p.m. the German representatives were ushered into a tent to sign the surrender of all the forces opposing the Allied Twenty-First Army Group, in effect, all German forces in north-western Germany, Holland and

Denmark. The actual surrender was recorded by the BBC, and broadcast to the world. Listeners heard Montgomery say in his distinctive clipped tone:

> Now we've assembled here today to accept the surrender terms which have been made with the delegation from the German Army. I will now read out the terms of that instrument of surrender. 'The German Command agrees to the surrender of all German forces in Holland, in north-west Germany, including the Friesian Islands and Heligoland and all other islands, in Schleswig-Holstein, and in Denmark to the Commander-in-Chief 21st Army Group. This is to include all naval ships in these areas. These forces to lay down their arms and to surrender unconditionally. All hostilities on land, on sea, or in the air by German forces in the above areas to cease at 0800 British Double Summer Time on Saturday 5 May, 1945.

Field Marshal Montgomery reads out the surrender terms to the German delegation prior to their signing. *(IWM BU5207)*

Then followed the signing, first by the German delegation led by Admiral von Friedeburg and General Kienzl. Montgomery ended, 'Now I will sign the instrument on behalf of the Supreme Allied Commander, General Eisenhower. Now that concludes the formal surrender and there are various matters now, or details to be discussed, which we will do in closed session.'

In this closed session, they began to discuss the bigger question of the surrender of the whole of Germany's armed forces on all fronts. General Eisenhower had agreed that, to this end, the German representatives should be brought to his headquarters in Rheims, on Saturday.

One familiar voice was missing from the radio; Lord Haw-Haw, the man who had broadcast German propaganda to Britain since the start of the war had been replaced by the BBC's Wynford Vaughan-Thomas. The familiar announcement of 'This is Germany calling, Germany calling', was followed by something different from the usual propaganda:

> Calling for the last time from Station Hamburg, and to-night you will not hear views on the news by William Joyce, for Mr Joyce – Lord Haw-Haw to most of us in Britain – has been most unfortunately interrupted in his broadcasting career, and at present has left rather hurriedly for a vacation, an extremely short vacation if the Second British Army has anything to do with it, maybe to Denmark and other points north.

In the south, the US Seventh Army captured Salzburg and Innsbrück, and Hitler's retreat at Berchtesgaden, and drove through the Brenner Pass into Italy.

## SATURDAY 5 MAY

Admiral Dönitz declared further resistance useless, and the German First and Nineteenth Armies in southern Germany surrendered. George Pringle was at the front:

> Although the war officially ended on 8 May, fighting in most parts ceased on the 5th. At that time I was with my regiment occupying a forward position on the River Elbe; we were told the war was over and given a bottle of beer each to celebrate the victory. The German troops were very

British troops of the 1st/5th Queen's Regiment entering Hamburg on 3 May, immediately after the surrender of the town. *(IWM BU5712)*

busy giving themselves up to us before the Russians arrived to take over the area from us as part of the agreement made at Yalta, so we had no time to celebrate as erecting barbed-wire compounds to house these thousands of prisoners of war gave us no free time.

Chief German negotiators, Admiral von Friedeburg, and Colonel Poleck, arrived at Eisenhower's HQ, and saw General Bedell Smith, Eisenhower's chief of staff, at a brief meeting, where it became clear that Friedeburg was not authorised to surrender. This authorisation was sought by telegraph, and this took several hours, at the end of which the Germans agreed to surrender all their forces in the west, but only to the western Allies. Clearly they intended at least some resistance against the Russians, to buy time to allow as many of their people as possible to escape to the west. However, Bedell Smith informed them that the Allies were prepared to accept nothing but unconditional surrender in the west simultaneously with unconditional surrender to the USSR. It was made clear that, failing this, the Allied lines in the west would be sealed off and no more Germans permitted to cross the lines as prisoners. The Germans were given forty-eight hours to come to a decision.

Meanwhile, the Russians captured Peenemünde, site of the V-bomb research station, while the British 7th Armoured Division crossed the Danish frontier and entered Jutland.

British officers arrive at the Hamburg Town Hall to take over the city from the general commanding the German garrison, following the surrender. *(IWM BU5723)*

In Britain speculation that the end might come at any minute was rife. The *News Chronicle* wrote:

> If someone had stood in the middle of Oxford Street yesterday and shouted 'This is V Day,' hundreds of Union Jacks would have appeared as if by magic . . . but no-one shouted, and the flags, purchased from barrows in the side-streets, remained furled or camouflaged as walking sticks.

The *Kentish Mercury* reported that:

Most of the public houses, cinemas and bigger shopping centres were already decorated in expectation of the great moment, and many houses in the little back streets had the bunting and flags flying in readiness. Groups of bewildered people stood talking in their doorways.

Anti-Nazi graffiti on the walls of war-damaged Hamburg houses, and friendly waves, greet advancing British forces, 4 May. *(IWM BU5376)*

## SUNDAY MAY 6

In the occupied Channel Islands, expectations were running at fever pitch; Union Jacks were openly on sale, and the Bailiff of Jersey, A.M. Coutanche, appealed to the civilian population for calm, urging that nothing should be done to provoke the German troops. Just after six o'clock news flashed round the islands that peace was imminent.

Alan Miles lived in Hall Green, Birmingham:

> Just prior to VE-Day, my dad, who was a policeman, came home from duty and said lots of roads were going to hold street parties with music and bonfires and as such Dunsmore Road should 'give it a good go'. He called on a few neighbours and it was all systems go. Dad told me to fetch my mates, all six-, seven- and eight-year-olds, to start collecting wood for a bonfire. After the first sortie we arrived back with a few twigs each; I remember him laughing and saying 'this is going to be a BIG bonfire', and so it was. What people brought out to be burned is nobody's business. The fire was built in the roadway almost opposite our house. It was massive.

Hamburg. Smashed German rifles and an empty champagne bottle eloquently and poignantly tell of the events of the last few hours before British troops arrived. *(IWM BU5297)*

The German Army Group G, comprising all German forces in Austria and southern Germany, surrendered to the US Sixth Army, and General Eisenhower's HQ in Rheims received word that Colonel-General Jodl, Deputy Chief of Staff of the German Armed Forces High Command, was on his way there by air.

## MONDAY 7 MAY

At 2.41 a.m., in a little red school-house in Rheims, Colonel-General Jodl, General Bedell Smith, Russian General Ivan Suslaparov, and French General François Sevez signed Germany's unconditional surrender to the Western Allies and the USSR. The German emissaries were repeatedly asked: 'Do you understand the significance and seriousness of the terms to which you are binding your country?', and each time they replied 'Yes, we do. Germany will carry them out.'

The text of the document stated:

1) We, the undersigned, acting by authority of the German High Command, hereby surrender unconditionally to the Supreme Commander, Allied Expeditionary Force, and simultaneously to the Soviet High Command of the Red Army, all forces on land, at sea and in the air who are this date under German control.

2) The German High Command will at once issue orders to all German military, naval and air authorities and to all forces under German control to cease active operations at 23.01 hours, Central European Time, on May 8, 1945, to remain in the positions occupied at that time, and to disarm completely, handing over their weapons and equipment to the local Allied commanders or officers designated by representatives of the Supreme Allied Commands. No ship, vessel or aircraft is to be scuttled or any damage done to their hulls, machinery or equipment, nor to machines of all kinds, armament, apparatus, and all the technical means of prosecution of war in general.

3) The German High Command will at once issue to the appropriate commanders and ensure the carrying out of, any further orders issued by the Supreme Commander, Allied Expeditionary Force, and by the Supreme High Command of the Red Army.

4) This act of military surrender is without prejudice to, and will be superseded by, any general instrument of surrender imposed by, or on behalf of, the United Nations and applicable to Germany and the German armed forces as a whole.

5) In the event of the German High Command or any of the forces under their control failing to act in accordance with this act of surrender the Supreme Commander, Allied Expeditionary Force, and the Supreme High Command of the Red Army will take such punitive or other action as they deem appropriate.

6) This act is drawn up in the English, Russian, and German languages. The English and Russian are the authentic texts.

After signing, General Jodl rose to his feet and said:

Some of the thousands of German prisoners taken as Lübeck fell, grateful to be in the hands of the Western Allies. Few, if any of them, did not believe by now that the war was over. *(IWM BU5206)*

General, with this signature the German people, and German armed forces are, for better or for worse, delivered into the victors' hands. In this war, which has lasted more than five years, both have achieved and suffered more than perhaps any other people in the world. In this hour I can only express the hope that the victor will treat them with generosity.

In Britain, there were long queues outside bakers' shops for bread – there would be few meals cooked over the next few days, sandwiches would be the thing for the VE celebrations; bakers worked all-night shifts and then worked through the day to keep pace with the demand. Shops soon sold out of bread, and sweets, and cakes; and there were other demands. Up and down the country men and women were clambering on ladders, hastily fixing flags and bunting. The *Mail* reported:

Toyshops, decorators, department shops and multiple stores brought out every red-white-and-blue piece of cloth to blaze their windows. Those flags not bought up by the prudent on Saturday were sold for anything up to a pound. In the streets hawkers were gaily a-flutter. A piece of bunting on a pole could fetch up to a £5 note, and there were more buyers than flags.

The *Liverpool Echo* noted that, 'Typists threaded their shoes with red-white-and-blue tape, throwing away the laces. Girls tore off their hats and scarves and tied up their hair in the colours of the flag.'

British and Soviet troops link up and celebrate. Note the 'liberated' Nazi ceremonial dagger in the belt of the British soldier second from right. *(IWM BU5235)*

At 1.25 p.m. the Danish Home Service gave a news flash that the surrender of the German forces in Norway had just been announced. In London, the first people began to assemble outside Buckingham Palace. They watched men refurbish the lanterns of the main gateway, while other workers refitted the wooden flooring of the King's balcony and electricians put finishing touches to the battery of floodlights in the palace forecourt. A trainer plane flew over, banking in the victory roll.

At 2.27 p.m., the new German Foreign Minister, Count Lutz Schwerin von Krosigk made a broadcast:

> German men and women: the High Command of the Armed Forces has today, at the order of Grand Admiral Dönitz, declared the unconditional surrender of all fighting German troops . . . No one must be under any illusions about the severity of the terms to be imposed on the German people by our enemies. We must now face our fate squarely and unquestioningly. Nobody can be in any doubt that the future will be difficult for each one of us, and will exact sacrifices from us in every sphere of life . . . In our nation justice shall be the supreme law and the guiding principle. We must also recognise law as the basis of all relations between the nations. We must recognise it and respect it from inner conviction. Respect for treaties will be as sacred as the aim of our nation to belong to the European family of nations, as a member of which we want to mobilise all human, moral and material forces in order to heal the dreadful wounds which the war has caused . . . May God not forsake us in our distress, and bless us in our heavy task.

At 3.45 a Reuters bulletin from Rheims announced that, 'The Allies today officially announced that Germany had surrendered unconditionally.' However, at 3.49 the German-controlled Prague Radio denounced von Krosigk's broadcast as 'enemy propaganda intent on breaking our troops' will to resist', and announced that they intended to fight on. 'The Reich government has only ceased to fight against the Western Powers', it added, 'In our area the struggle will be continued until the Germans of the east are saved and until our way back into the homeland is secured.' At 3.55 (British time), however, New York Radio reported details of the signing.

The British afternoon papers reported that morning's events; the crowd outside Buckingham palace continued to grow, as did expectations. The steps of Queen Victoria's memorial became black with people. Papers were snapped up and those lucky enough to get them were surrounded by crowds eager to hear the latest news.

Hamburg – In a reflection of earlier scenes in France, and other places, German civilians read the orders of the British Military Government. *(IWM BU5416)*

Peter Baker remembered:

In 1945 I was a member of 1079 Squadron ATC [Air Training Corps] based in Tiverton, Devon, on detachment at RNAS Yeovilton for a week's introduction to service life on an air station. Up to Monday 7 May all our activities had gone according to programme. That day progressed in an orderly manner but as the day wore on there was an undercurrent of rumour amongst the sailors and wrens. 'Is the war over?' 'Don't know.' 'They say the war in Europe is over.' 'There may be an announcement tonight.' 'Not long to demob.' 'I hope so.' And so it went on.

There might as yet be no official announcement of victory, but Churchill gave a special victory luncheon party in the garden of 10 Downing Street.

The guests were the Chiefs of Staff, including Sir Charles Portal (RAF), Sir Alan Brooke (Army), Sir Andrew Cunningham (Navy), Major-General Hollis (Secretary to the Chiefs of Staff Committee), and General Sir Hastings Ismay, Churchill's personal chief of staff. The Prime Minister toasted them as 'the architects of victory'.

After lunch, Churchill was ready to broadcast, but no news of Washington's or Moscow's assent had been received. During the afternoon Churchill tried to persuade Truman to make the announcement of victory that evening, but the President refused, saying that Stalin wanted to wait until the 9th, as his forces were still fighting in Czechoslovakia and parts of the Baltic.

There were some official announcements. Sheltering in the London underground was now discontinued; it was estimated that, since September 1940, 50 million people had taken refuge there. The Board of Trade did its bit for the celebrations, 'Until the end of May you may buy cotton bunting without coupons, as long as it is red, white or blue and does not cost more than 1s 3d [6p] a quarter yard.'

In spite of victory, stocks and shares were down. Actually there was little trading that day, with many brokers, anticipating the victory announcement, being absent. It was reported that, 'Owing to the absence of buyers, greater emphasis was given to post-war political and other uncertainties and dealers adopted the usual precaution of marking down prices.'

It was not only German forces that seemed unclear as to the surrender; just after 5.30, the US Transradio News Service broadcast the following: 'SHAEF [Supreme Headquarters Allied Expeditionary Force] authorises correspondents to state that SHAEF has nowhere made any official statement for publication up to 4.45 p.m. concerning the complete surrender of all the German forces in Europe, and any story to that effect is unauthorised.' Three-quarters of an hour later, Paris Radio commented, 'It is probable that the announcement of capitulation will be delayed until fighting ceases everywhere. It is also probable that it will be issued simultaneously in Moscow, London, New York and Paris.'

Meanwhile, in St Paul's Cathedral, twelve elderly men stood waiting for hours on end to ring the bells in a peal of triumph. Outside the cathedral a growing crowd also waited to thank God for victory. The *Daily Sketch* reported that the lack of an official announcement 'led to a good deal of confusion, premature rejoicing and mystification'. Churchill himself was still trying to change Truman's mind. At 5.00 he called the president again, telling him that the crowds in London were 'beyond control', and that he must make an announcement by noon of the following day at the latest. As Churchill's call suggests, official announcement or not, the people were taking over. The *Sketch* continued:

> Flags came out and excited crowds lined Whitehall. There was singing and dancing in the streets. Planes crossed and re-crossed London, doing the victory roll but, although the nation waited expectantly to hear Mr Churchill, there was no official announcement here.

A squadron of American Flying Fortress bombers flew over London, to a huge cheer from the crowd. Notices went up in American Red Cross Clubs that all leave passes would be given a forty-eight hour extension.

The British Ambassador to France, Duff Cooper, wrote in his diary that day:

> General Redmond (who among his other duties acted as my liaison officer with SHAEF) came to see me this morning and told me that the unconditional surrender of Germany had been signed in the early hours of this morning at Rheims. He also said that the news was not to be divulged. This last I said was nonsense. The declaration of war was bungled in 1939 and the announcement of unconditional surrender was being bungled now in 1945. However it is great news.

In Bath:

> People started celebrating VE-Day on Monday evening – many in fact commenced in the afternoon when the news became known. Faces lit up when the *Bath and Wilts Chronicle* appeared on the streets and papers sold like wildfire. Flags appeared on the city streets on Monday afternoon. Many people hung out flags and emblems they had saved from the coronation. Newsboys on Monday afternoon were shouting 'Victory Paper' instead of their usual 'War News, Latest!' One man celebrated too soon,' said Detective Inspector T. Coles at Bath Magistrates Court when John

Two German soldiers on their way to surrender to the British, families in tow. Surrender to the British or US forces meant safety from the Russians. *(IWM 5730)*

McIlmurray of Hawthorn was charged with being drunk and incapable in Southgate Street at 3 o'clock on Monday afternoon.

Mrs Sewell remembered:

I was doing some shopping for mum at the dairy on the corner. On my way home, I had just turned the corner into our street, Tilton Street, off Lily Road, Fulham, when all of a sudden people came running out into the street shouting that the war was over. I rushed in to mum to tell her – we went out into the street – people were kissing and hugging each other.

John Wheatley was in Torquay:

I was working for a builder on a private house, and the old toff who owned it told us the war was over. The house was close to a large secondary school, that day we heard a great cheer go up, presumably the pupils were assembled in the playground and had been told the good news.

The tension mounted. Rumours abounded; the news would be announced at three, then at four, then at six – just in time for the BBC News! But each deadline passed, and there was nothing but a bigger crowd. It was the same throughout the country. In village pubs, in the streets, everyone was discussing the same thing; when would the announcement be made. The usual suspects had the inside information, of course, they had it on first class authority, they had had a phone call from London, the big news was coming at some time in the afternoon or evening. People listened to the wireless for a sudden bulletin.

Allied prisoners of war in Oflag 79, Brunswick, swarm the gates as troops of the US Ninth Army arrive to free them, 12 April. *(IWM BU5985)*

The *Daily Mail* of 8 May reported:

Until shortly before 6 o'clock last night it was fully expected that Mr Churchill would be able to announce the news that the war was over. He had been standing by the microphone from some time after 3 o'clock, and everything was ready for him to break into the normal programmes of the B.B.C. Earlier in the day he had been speaking on the transatlantic telephone to Washington, and he also had several calls to Moscow. His object was to obtain an agreed time for releasing the big news. It was nearly 6 o'clock when it was learned that both the United States and the Soviet government were in favour of postponing the formal announcing until this afternoon.

At 8 o'clock that evening, in an amazing piece of officialese worthy of *Yes, Minister*'s Sir Humphrey, the Ministry of Information issued an announcement that the Prime Minister would broadcast the official announcement of the end of hostilities in Europe the following day at 3 p.m. Tuesday 8 May would, therefore, be treated as Victory in Europe Day, and the day following would also be a bank holiday. The King would broadcast, to the peoples of the British Empire and Commonwealth, at 9 p.m.

For most, this was confirmation enough. The *Daily Sketch* next day reported:

At dusk last night I went for a slow cruise through the jammed streets of the West End. It was like cleaving a passage through jungle – an uproarious human jungle which slowly swayed and circled under its own panoply of Union Jacks large and small. Victory, said London to herself, is here, under our noses, in our hearts. All this business of 'announcing' victory or 'proclaiming' it with wigs and parchments is slightly unreal. We're going to celebrate victory now. And celebrate it London did. Thousands flocked to town after the first pause of perplexity and disappointment. Their wish was for spontaneous revelry – not for high jinx taken out of cold store the morning after.

Peter Baker:

. . . at 7.30 p.m. the Tannoy burst into life with the never to be forgotten announcement, 'The war in Europe is over'. 8 May 1945 is VE-Day, with the 8th and 9th May being holidays. Winston Churchill would broadcast to the nation at 3.00 p.m. on VE-Day. In the camp cinema the film was interrupted to flash up notice of the cessation of the war in Europe, which was followed by an enormous cheer. We ATC cadets had been having tea and wads in the NAAFI at that time, immediately the sailors and wrens cheered, laughed, consumed more beer and began planning tomorrow's celebrations.

Ships on the Thames began to sound their sirens. The *Kentish Mercury* reported, 'The river shipping shrieked its paean of praise as it had not done since that far-off New Year's Eve of 1938.' Dorothy Richardson had lived in Queen's Park until she married early in the war when she moved to New Cross in south-east London, near the Thames; she had never heard river celebrations:

I remember my husband was on leave, and of course, along the water all the hooters were going, and I said to him 'What's all the noise?' and he said 'That's all the hooters along the water, haven't you never seen them?' I said 'No' so he said 'Come on we'll go, I'll take you to Greenwich.' I had some money I was saving up for some furniture after the war, so I put it in my pocket. He said we'd need to catch a bus: 'Oh, Damn, I haven't got any money.' 'I have', I said, and when I looked in my pocket it had gone – I'd pulled my handkerchief out to wipe the baby's nose and I'd lost it. So we never got to the river, but I could hear it. It was so exciting, everybody was smiling again.

The river salute went on for two hours.

Even after the official announcement a crowd still hung on outside Number Ten. Then there was a sudden shout, 'Here he comes!' The crowd pressed forward round a car, inside which sat a single passenger, Winston Churchill, smiling broadly and smoking his customary cigar, exchanging beams with the shouting crowd and giving his V-sign.

For some the news was received philosophically – it had been six years coming, another day would not matter. The *Liverpool Echo* reported:

The red, white, and blue fluttered triumphantly out of household windows very soon after the official news was known that to-day was to be VE-Day, and the loudspeaker relays of speeches and music for dancing gave an ultra-modern touch to the celebrations everywhere. Birkenhead people for the most part spent the last daylight hours in preparation for to-day's official celebration, and this activity was the main sign of jollification. The town was quickly transformed from its everyday normal appearance into a veritable blaze of colour. From every house flags of all nationalities, bunting, streamers, and the like were flown and draped from windows. Several streets produced effigies of Hitler, complete with scaffold. Hundreds gathered in front of the Town Hall to watch corporation electricians applying the finishing touches to the illuminations that are to be a feature of the town's Victory celebrations.

But for some, especially the young, there was no time to waste. The *Glasgow Herald* described the evening as 'a festival of youth'. The *Daily Mail* commented, 'The people of London, denied VE-Day officially, held their own jubilation. "VE-Day may be to-morrow," they said, "but the war is over to-night."'

Crowds appeared from nowhere on the streets of London; a seemingly unending stream poured forth from the underground stations as thousands travelled 'up west' for the celebrations. Buckingham Palace became the great converging point. The *London Evening News* reported, 'As soon as the news spread through London, many thousands of Londoners, moved by the same thought, began to move in the same direction. They began to move towards the Palace. They wanted to cheer the King.' A *Daily Sketch* reporter was there, too:

Shortly after 10 p.m. my car cautiously inched its way down Pall Mall towards a constellation of newly-lighted lamps at the Admiralty Arch. We had to make our way through a wide and solid stream of hilarious citizenry. Most of them were young people. It looked as though most of the youth clubs of London had been convoked for a genial mass march upon the home of Royalty. Fifteen abreast, they came with a sizeable Union Jack held aloft by a youth in the middle of the front rank. As they marched they chanted rhythmically:

> One, two, three, four,
>  What are we waiting for?
>  Five, six, seven, eight,
>  To-morrow will be far too late.

The invading column marched round and round the Victoria memorial which in the last light of Victory Day, was a swarm of humanity. It marched between the memorial and a dense crowd which spread into the roadway from the Palace railings. Cheers were exchanged. The chant of impatience was repeated, with interludes of popular songs.

Yet it was not all wild celebrations, as the *Evening News* noted:

Throughout the dusk a constant and reverent stream of men and women passed round the Cenotaph. They were queuing to pay homage to the dead of thirty years ago.

For a moment they had set their rejoicing aside. Young and old were there – Britons, Allied men from the ends of the earth. They moved slowly round the shaft of solemn stone. They were an island of recollection, an oasis of fidelity in the endless expanse of a nation's joy. For me the Cenotaph, Whitehall, at dusk will be the most enduring memory of Surrender Day.

By the time darkness fell it was estimated that there were at least 12,000 people outside the Palace, impatient to hear victory announced. There were cheers when lights were turned on, and when members of the palace staff appeared on the roof, a shout went up – 'We want the King!' Eventually there was great disappointment when word went round that due to the postponement of the announcement, the King and Queen would not make any public appearance that night.

By now The Mall was jammed, and police were diverting traffic from there and from the precincts of the palace. In Piccadilly Circus, too, the rostrum and hoarding where Eros had stood was thickly crowded, the pavements were jammed, and most of the roadways were impassable, while in Regent Street, buses were having to be diverted. The *Sketch* reported, 'Buses laboured slowly through the throng like trawlers making for port in heavy weather. Passengers waved their flags through the windows. The people below waved back.'

Of course London was not the only place which was celebrating that night; Roy Proctor was working as a trainee operator at the Ritz Cinema in Felixstowe:

Crowds in Piccadilly watching planes performing aerobatics to celebrate news of the German surrender, 7 May. *(IWM HU92007)*

I was working until 9pm; when I came out there was a large crowd and an army band was playing 'When the lights go on again all over the world', everyone was singing along with it, and then some of the street lights came on!

The *Bath and Wilts Chronicle* recorded that, 'Public houses in the city and district were crowded on Monday night. For most of them it was "beer only".'

The *Daily Mail* takes up the story:

The last trains departed from the West End unregarded. The pent-up spirits of the throng, the polyglot throng that is London in war-time, burst out, and by 11 o'clock the capital was ablaze with enthusiasm.

Processions formed up out of nowhere, disintegrating for no reason, to re-form somewhere else. Waving flags, marching in step, with linked arms or half-embraced, the people strode through the great thoroughfares – Piccadilly, Regent Street, The Mall, to the portals of Buckingham Palace.

They marched and counter-marched so as not to get too far from the centre. And from them, in harmony and discord, rose song. The songs of the last war, the songs of a century ago, the songs of the beginning of this war: 'Roll out the Barrel' and 'Tipperary'; 'Ilkla Moor' and 'Loch Lomond'; 'Bless 'em All' and 'Pack Up Your Troubles'. London University students formed a mile-long procession that traipsed up and down the Strand.

And many had missed those last trains; often on purpose. It was a warm day and fortified by a mixture of alcohol and high spirits, mostly high spirits, they had vowed to stay in the parks overnight so as not to miss a thing in the morning.

As the night wore on, some of the celebrating threatened to get out of control. A debris fire began to rage in an excavation off Shaftesbury Avenue, and the flames threatened adjoining property. A National Fire Service (NFS) crew turned out and dealt with it, but when they returned through Piccadilly the fire engine was besieged by a cheering crowd including servicemen of half a dozen nations, many of whom climbed aboard. However, the NFS managed to struggle through eventually.

In Panton Street a crowd overturned two cars, but British and American soldiers went to the rescue, and the cars were righted. In Coventry Street someone stole a soldier's bayonet in the crush and used it to pierce the petrol tank of a waiting car. Then somebody threw a lighted match on to the leaking petrol and in seconds the car was blazing. Police had to charge the crowd to move them away.

Bonfires, officially allowed for VE-Day, were definitely not allowed that night, but no one much took any notice. The *Evening News* reported that, 'London was ringed with bonfires by midnight. Rejoicing crowds in the East End and other suburbs lit them on bomb sites that had been cleared and wherever there was an open space.' The *Kentish Mercury* noted that they were, 'fuelled from some mysterious but inexhaustible source'. The *Daily Mail* reported that, 'On Hampstead Hill a huge throng gathered to look down over London. And one woman who had lost the irreplaceable in the blitz, looked out over London across the glaring lights and murmured: "I never want to see London glow again – even to-night."'

The VE-Day issue of the *Liverpool Echo* commented:

Last night there were premature bonfire blazes, and the N.F.S. had to turn out to quench about five of them. Officially bonfires were illegal last night and will be again tomorrow night. Many N.F.S. units in Liverpool celebrated VE eve by turning out to false fire calls. 'Malicious merry-makers who kept on calling us from street boxes had a gay time,' one official told the *Echo*. 'Their sense of fun is not appreciated by the fire-fighters.'

The *Daily Mail* also described some troubles:

In the early hours the rough stuff became somewhat rougher. Young university students started tearing down cinema hoardings in Coventry Street and the Haymarket and making bonfires of them. For the first time the police had to 'take steps'. The first bonfire was lit outside the Gaumont Cinema. Boys and girls danced round it, whooping and cheering. After a few minutes of this a smiling police sergeant pushed his way through the crowd and told the ringleaders to stop tearing down the hoardings. He also moved people away. Further evidence of rowdyism was shown in broken traffic lights – people had wrenched off what was left of the black-out masks, and many of the safety lights on the road islands were damaged.

Next day's *London Evening News*, however, stated that, 'Scotland Yard reported that it was "very gratified" by the crowd's behaviour, stating that no charges had been bought in connection with the celebrations, and that there had been no trouble in the area, apart from two bonfires "which for a time caused a little concern".'

As midnight approached police estimated that over 50,000 people were packed into Piccadilly Circus and the roads leading to it. To prevent the situation from becoming worse they stopped all traffic from approaching the area. And the crowds and the noise grew; people sang wildly, or cheered as something gained their attention. Near Leicester Square a pile of straw filled with thunder-flashes salvaged from some military dump spurted and exploded. Hooters and whistles were blowing and every five minutes detonators were fired; there were the noises of gas rattles (once used to warn against gas), and music from radios, records, and bands. 'In the middle of

Piccadilly Circus a man stood under the traffic lights playing an accordion.' In Deptford they were 'dancing in the street to the music of accordions, barrel organ, and hastily improvised and often novel "orchestras".' And there were fireworks; every minute or so fireworks were let off. 'Rockets – found no one knows where, set off by no one knows whom – streaked into the sky.' There were even coloured flares, dropped by aircraft.

In London, just after 1.30 a.m. a 'tropical storm' broke out. It was estimated by many to be the worst since that of the night of 2–3 September 1939; and it was in some way fitting that a war, ushered in by a violent storm, should finish with one. The *Evening News* reported that the storm 'left pools of water across low-lying land in various parts of London. Wooden road blocks were forced up in Shaftesbury Avenue by the rush of water. Many late night victory revellers in the West End were caught by the storm, and hundreds sought shelter in doorways, where they were marooned for hours.' Those who had decided to sleep out in the parks had a hard night of it. The storm continued with vivid streaks of lightning and crashing rolls of thunder until after 4 a.m. A house in Addison Road, Kensington, was struck by lightning, and NFS men later had to demolish its chimney.

Yet the storm did little to dampen the revellers' enthusiasm. The *Kentish Mercury* reported that in Blackheath, 'They got soaked almost to the skin, the Mayor among them, but still the merry-making went on, to finish in the early hours of the long-awaited VE-Day itself.'

In spite of the lack of official news, people all over the world had begun celebrating peace in Europe. In New York, too, tens of thousands took an unofficial holiday. The news from Rheims reached there at breakfast-time. Vast crowds thronged the streets, and ticker-tape, ripped-up telephone directories, and waste-paper baskets were showered down from skyscrapers around Times Square. Celebrations continued unabated all day, despite the plethora of confusing official announcements, as the *Daily Mail* reported:

For hours upon hours, tons of ticker-tape, torn-up newspapers, envelopes, letters, magazines and in some cases hats and waste-paper baskets, cascaded down. Tens of thousands of people abandoned work and rushed into the Times Square area, shouting and singing. Motorists blew their hooters, factory whistles shrieked, and in New York Bay ships sounded

Despite the lack of any official announcement, the evening of 7 May witnessed the start of the celebrations of peace, in this case on the roof of a London taxi. *(IWM HU92008)*

their sirens. Bands of servicemen and girls paraded the avenues waving flags, shouting and yelling, planting kisses on strangers, cavorting in and out of bars. Great stores, offices, the banks and factories closed down as staffs walked out en masse. Traffic was completely tied up in mid-town as throngs of gesticulating, laughing people jammed roadways, jumped on to the running boards of private cars, taxis, and buses. At first city officials, led by Mayor La Guardia, attempted to curb the jubilation. Over the radio came a reminder that there was nothing official, that it was merely a report which had declared that war in Europe was over. The people ignored the advice.

Although liberated, most of the Allied prisoners of war behind the Russian lines had not been moved out, as Leslie Kerridge recalled:

We had been released now and could not understand why we were being kept in Stalag IVB. We were all very naturally anxious to be on our way home but the Russians did not seem to be giving us the slightest thought. They were very friendly in a rough and ready sort of way but that was to be expected from such a tough army.

We at last received orders from the Russians to be ready to move at short notice. We still had to wait another two days during which time we had a visit from some Americans who rode into the camp on a jeep. We had been in the camp fourteen days since our release when we at last heard that we were to proceed on foot to a fairly large town called Reisa about twenty miles from the camp. At last we left Stalag IVB behind us and I think that we all breathed a sigh of relief to see it slowly recede into the distance. During our march we saw evidence of action having taken place, and in one small village it looked as though quite a battle had been fought out. We passed many convoys of Russian transport and had cigarettes and cigars showered at us.

In neutral Dublin, however, the news was the signal for an outbreak of fighting! Trinity College students hoisted the Union Jack and the Red Flag over the university, singing 'God Save the King' and 'Rule Britannia'. Onlookers booed and jeered, and scuffles broke out, causing the Garda to intervene. Eventually they had to baton-charge the angry crowd which had gathered, and several were taken to hospital, while students wearing college scarves were attacked in the streets, and some university windows broken.

In Lisbon crowds thronged into the squares carrying British and US flags, while in Oslo street loudspeakers which for the last five years had relayed Nazi propaganda suddenly proclaimed 'Peace!' Immediately the streets began to fill with men and women, singing the Norwegian national anthem, political prisoners were set free from the jails, by police and prison guards who suddenly 'lost' their 'quisling' uniforms. In Brazil, President Vargas proclaimed a national holiday in celebration of victory, while in the Vatican City, the bells of St Peter's rang out 'Victory' chimes on the order of the Vatican authorities.

# CHAPTER 4

# VE-Day

## CELEBRATIONS BEGIN

This is the Day of Days. We have waited a long time for it, and now celebrate in joyful manner. Go to it and enjoy yourselves.

*Liverpool Echo*, 8 May

Some started celebrating at midnight, as recorded by the *Glasgow Herald*:

No sooner had midnight struck than the ships on the Clyde started to herald the victory. The vessels at the anchorage of Greenock and Gourock and alongside the quays commenced with the sounding of the 'V' signal. Soon it was taken up by the other ships, and in a few moments there was the greatest cacophony of sound ever heard in the area. The sounding of sirens was followed almost immediately by the flashing of searchlights from naval ships and soon the whole sky was stabbed by pencils of light.

Caernarvon was also awakened at midnight by loud noises, although in this case a passing military convoy proved to be the cause. It had halted in Castle Square, and the troops decided to celebrate victory with a half hour of

*The Strip that Sums Up the Situation: Jane Celebrates Victory in the Only Way She Knows*

Here the *Daily Mirror*'s own Jane, from 8 May, celebrates victory by losing her clothes – well, some things had to carry on as usual!

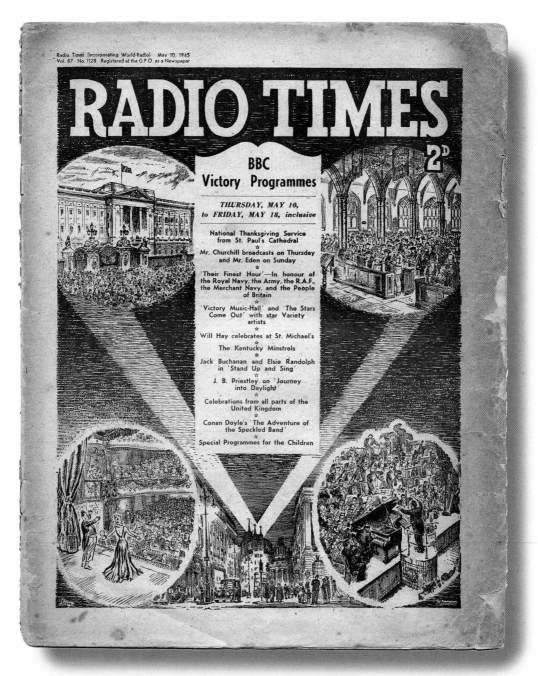

Radio Times (incorporating World-Radio) May 10, 1945
Vol. 87 No. 1128 Registered at the G.P.O. as a Newspaper

# RADIO TIMES

2D

## BBC
## Victory Programmes

*THURSDAY, MAY 10,
to FRIDAY, MAY 18, inclusive*

National Thanksgiving Service
from St. Paul's Cathedral
✦
Mr. Churchill broadcasts on Thursday
and Mr. Eden on Sunday
✦
'Their Finest Hour'—In honour of
the Royal Navy, the Army, the R.A.F.,
the Merchant Navy, and the People
of Britain
✦
'Victory Music-Hall' and 'The Stars
Come Out' with star Variety
artists
✦
Will Hay celebrates at St. Michael's
✦
The Kentucky Minstrels
✦
Jack Buchanan and Elsie Randolph
in 'Stand Up and Sing'
✦
J. B. Priestley on 'Journey
into Daylight'
✦
Celebrations from all parts of the
United Kingdom
✦
Conan Doyle's 'The Adventure of
the Speckled Band'
✦
Special Programmes for the Children

Cover of the *Radio Times* 'Victory Edition'. The articles had been prepared for some time but, even so, the selection of victory programmes was a masterpiece of improvisation considering the muddle over the announcement of the actual victory.

thunderflashes, which caused a terrific din and illuminated the neighbourhood.

Admiral Dönitz, Hitler's chosen successor, broadcast to the German nation:

In my first speech to the German people on 1 May, I declared it was my task to save German lives. I cannot tell you whether I shall be able to help the German people. We must face the hard facts of the present situation. The Nazi Party has disappeared. There is no longer unity between the state and party. The foundations on which the German Reich were built no longer exist. From 23.00 Central European Time on 8 May, the guns will be silent . . . There is a difficult road ahead for every one of us. We must tread it with the dignity, gallantry and discipline which the memory of our dead demands . . . We may tread the road in the hope that the time will come when our children will live a free and secure life in a Europe at peace.

The German-controlled Prague Radio announced at 6.15 a.m. that, after defying their High Command's orders for twenty-four hours, a cease-fire order had been given to the local German troops at 1.30 a.m. Elsewhere it was announced that the body of Josef Goebbels, Germany's Propaganda Minister, and those of his wife and five children had been found in an air-raid shelter near the Reichstag, and that all had died of poisoning. There was much speculation as to the whereabouts of Göring, and far more importantly Hitler. Other news included the freeing of such prominent anti-Nazis as Pastor Niemoller, Dr Schuschnigg, ex-Chancellor of Austria, and Leon Blum, former socialist Prime Minister of France

In Britain, newspapers were able to give the first weather forecasts since 1939 (they had been banned almost as soon as war broke out under the heading of 'giving information which might be of use to the enemy'). This was, for many, the first real evidence of the return of peace-time habits. It is strange to think how the words: 'Sunny and warm at first with the wind freshening; probably becoming cloudy with rain later' could be such a joy.

Even for those unable or unwilling to join in the fun, there was always the wireless. Programmes for that day on the Home Service included:

| | |
|---|---|
| 3.00 | The Prime Minister |
| 3.10 | Thanksgiving Service from Cardington |
| 3.20 | Victory Celebration Bells |
| 4.00 | Band of the Royal Horse Guards |
| 4.30 | BBC Midland Light Orchestra |

7.00    Joe Loss and his Orchestra

7.30    BBC Symphony Orchestra

8.00    Thanksgiving Service and
        Address by the Archbishop
        of Canterbury

8.30    Tribute to the King

9.00    His Majesty the King:
        News and Victory Report

2.00    Closedown

In a strange way this summed up the day itself beautifully; momentous and solemn events, interspersed by light music, going on until late.

The *Radio Times* 'Special Victory Issue' put it rather differently:

The mood of this unforgettable hour will be reflected in the BBC programmes. Through the miracle of radio, listeners in Britain and overseas will be able to share their emotions; they will be active participants in rejoicings that will ring round the world. The dominant feeling must be one of thankfulness. There will be no mafficking: the people of Britain are too conscious of the cost of this most terrible of all wars to indulge in that — too well aware of the sternness and difficulties of the task that still faces them. But they would not be human if they did not give expression to feelings of joy and pride: joy at the return of peace to a large part of the war-wracked world, pride in the achievements of the Allied armies. So the bells will ring, toasts will be drunk, happy crowds will surge in the streets . . .

Microphones set up all over the country and linked by an intricate network of lines to a focal point in London will bring to the listener eye-witness accounts of what is happening. Without leaving his armchair he

## Scotch Eggs—new style
### *Tasty, nourishing, and easy to make with dried eggs*

**Just one of the** many tempting dishes you can make with dried eggs — that old favourite, Scotch Eggs!

Make hard-boiled eggs by reconstituting the dried eggs and pouring into a greased egg-cup or mould — one egg to a mould. Then steam in a pan of simmering (*not* boiling) water for 10 or 15 minutes, until it sets. Turn out of the mould by slipping a knife round the edge.

*Hard-boiled eggs*

**This** gives you excellent hard-boiled eggs, for dried eggs *are* shell eggs — new-laid ones—with only shell and water removed, and they have exactly the same nutritional value as

shell eggs. No need to worry about the egg shortage with dried eggs in the house!

For every four "hard-boiled eggs" allow half a pound of sausage meat. Cut the meat into four portions and flatten to a circle about half an inch thick. Fold a circle of meat over each hard-boiled egg, covering it completely, dip in a reconstituted egg, then roll in breadcrumbs and fry till golden brown.

There's no end to the delicious dishes you can make with dried eggs. Omelettes and scrambled eggs are always favourites.

*No end of delicious egg dishes with dried eggs!*

DE18    ISSUED BY THE MINISTRY OF FOOD, LONDON, W.1

Even the Ministry of Food hints had a party feel in May 1945, such as this one for Scotch eggs.

will be able to move from Piccadilly to Princes Street, from Bedford to Belfast, from Cornwall to Cardiff. He will hear the joy-bells peal from St Paul's, from the great Midland cathedrals, from remote country churches. He will mingle with the victory crowds on city pavements, in village streets, in churches, in dance-halls, in theatres.

Microphones have been installed at many points where something of interest is likely to occur. In London alone, more than fifty have been installed, and at three points – in the Green Park, in Downing Street, and in Piccadilly – commentators and recording engineers will be on duty, night and day, throughout the twenty-four hours. In addition, six recording vans will be moving about in the London area and a mobile transmitter installed in a car will 'flash' material to headquarters by way of two specially arranged receiving points in Central London.

Flags and bunting appeared from attics and cellars; some from the Coronation in 1937. Putting out the flags for the victory celebrations in Aberdeen.

## YOUR VE-GUIDE TODAY

All workers except those on essential services have their VE-day holiday to-day. Here is a guide to plans and events.

The bells of St Paul's and other churches will ring out at intervals all day. All churches are open for prayer. At St Paul's the Lord Mayor, Sir Frank Alexander, will attend the Thanksgiving service.

Cinemas in the West End will be closed, but suburban cinemas are open.

Theatres are open.

Searchlights will give a display from 11.45 p.m. until 12.15 a.m. over Central London and the suburbs.

Public houses in the London area have been given extensions, but during the day the hours will be as usual.

Dance Halls are open – in some cases until 3 a.m.

Schools are closed.

Banks, open until midday, are possibly staying open later.

Post Offices are closed, except those maintaining a 24-hour service. No collections or deliveries.

Flood Lighting: Public buildings in London, including Buckingham Palace, Whitehall and the Houses of Parliament, will be floodlit.

Taxis won't be seen, unless you are lucky.

Police: All on duty, with the three days off later.

Law Courts: King's Bench judges sitting, but may rise early.

London Stock Exchange: Closed.

Museums: Closed.                    Art Galleries: Closed.

Zoo: Open.                          Royal Academy: Open

Bonfires will be lit at many places. Your black-out, no longer needed, can go on the flames, but keep your gas mask.

Street Lighting: Streets will be lit to-night.

In the streets of large towns and cities, hastily produced local programmes were distributed. This is an extract from the 'VE-Day Illuminations Souvenir Programme' for London:

*Opposite:* Fleet Street adorned with flags and ticker tape. *(IWM HU92006)*

Prominent Buildings Illuminated: Big Ben, The Houses of Parliament, Buckingham Palace, St Paul's Cathedral, Nelson's Column and all Town Halls in London.

Searchlight Display: London Region H.Q. will give a searchlight display over Central London to-night from 11.45 p.m. to 12.15 a.m. and again tomorrow night during the same hour.

## MORNING

The early morning of VE-Day was quiet after the previous evening's revelry. Here and there people were out making final preparations for the day's events, putting up the last bit of bunting or getting tables out for their street party.

Jenny D'Eath recalled that in Norfolk, 'Everyone put flags, coloured sheets, or anything bright, out of the windows.' Flags, of course, made up the main decorations. The *Liverpool Echo* recorded that, 'Colonel Beazley, a former High Sheriff of Chester, hoisted on the tower the new victory flag which he has presented to the cathedral. Never has Chester been so beflagged.' In the centre of Chester's main shopping area, alongside a huge V, were printed the words 'From Dunkirk to Victory,' surrounded by Union Jacks and the flags of all the other Allied nations. The *Liverpool Echo*:

> There were few streets in Wallasey to-day without a display of flags, banners and bunting, householders and shopkeepers alike having readily fallen in with the official suggestion that there should be a liberal display of the emblem of victory and rejoicing.

Or in Wales, again according to the *Liverpool Echo*:

> The display of flags in Denbigh and Ruthin surpasses anything previously seen in those towns. The Union Jack and Welsh Dragon flags have been hoisted on public buildings and on the historic castles, and miniatures on every house. The streets are profusely decorated and there is an atmosphere of joyous elation.

And, the *Echo* reported, there were similar scenes in a host of different places all around the country:

There were flags of all the United Nations, from great banners flying proudly over the Town Hall, all other civic centres, and the large commercial houses and stores, to tiny colours no larger than a pocket handkerchief, but conveying, for all their lack of size, an equally patriotic spirit.

Buildings were draped with streamers in red, white and blue, and Union Jacks, or combining the national colours of the nations sharing in this memorable victory. A favourite banner was a composite representation of the British and American colours. There were the flags of all the dominions, and vast V signs in some cases stretching from the cornice almost to the footpath. In the outer districts flags were also flying, and in some areas where working people live the decorations were astonishingly elaborate. At one point, two little Chinese flags fluttered, and the Chinese quarter had its banners, too. Considering that the supply of bunting available in shops and stores has not been great, the display was astonishing.

In dock areas, ships, tugs and ferryboats were also decorated, with most covering themselves with banners and flags. 'As one large ship moved slowly up the river, dressed gaily with bunting, the passengers on a ferry-boat cheered and waved, and sailors cheered back in return.' The *Scotsman* reported that in Leith, 'All the ships in port had flags flying, and a number carried "rainbow" decorations, the whole giving a gay appearance to the harbour and docks.'

The *Kentish Mercury* commented:

They rummaged their cellars and attics and brought out a wealth of bunting which had served as a national expression of joy on another auspicious occasion – the coronation of King George VI. There were flags and streamers of every description; symbols and signals mattered not a jot: colour, gaiety was the order of the day. Union Jacks, perhaps, predominated, they occupied exalted and honoured positions – but the star-spangled banner, the hammer and sickle on its blood-red field, the national emblems of many countries, red and white ensigns and scores of other flags, bedecked the streets. It made one wonder, where in these days of rigid austerity, they all came from . . .

Celebrations in Queen Victoria Square, Hull, 10 May. Hull had been badly hit by the bombing, as can be seen by the bomb sites surrounding the square.

In a twinkling, or so it seemed, the flags of the Allies were flying from a thousand places, giant 'Vs' were festooning the fronts of bombed, scarred houses, and some of the more ingenious had erected the sign of victory in scintillating fairy lights, synchronised to send their message in the dot-dot-dot-dash that Europe had come to know as the signal of its coming liberation.

Lights, so long banned under the black-out, became a central part of many decorations. In Croydon, 'Bright illuminations were devised by the Electricity Department for the Town Hall, Katherine Street and the Town Hall gardens.' In Bebbington, 'Fairy lights and flood lights have been erected in readiness for tonight,' while 'Southport's famous Lord Street was gaily decorated today with bunting which will be augmented tonight when fairy lights in the trees will be switched on for the first time in nearly six years.'

In Stockport, Corporation buses carried huge letter 'V's' with Churchill's photograph in the middle, while in the village of Upper Weston a large 'V' sign was erected which contained a picture of Winston Churchill surmounted by the words 'Weston Thanks You'.

Churchill himself was working in bed on his victory broadcast, stopping to check that there were adequate supplies of beer in the capital for the night's celebrations. Most pubs and bars up and down the country had been granted extensions to midnight.

As usual for what was, effectively, a Bank Holiday, passenger transport provision was switched to Sunday services for the two-day holiday, but, like much of the other information about VE-Day and VE plus 1 this was only announced at the last minute. In the previous evening's midnight news, it had been announced that: 'London Transport underground railways, central buses and trams and trolley-buses will run ordinary Sunday services.' It was then repeated at 7 and 8 o'clock that morning, but even so, many people who had to work that day arrived late at their offices. In the capital, there were long queues in some of the inner suburbs and central districts for the normal early buses; there were no taxis on the streets and few civilian cars and no commercial lorries to give lifts.

People living in the areas covered by the country services were also caught out, believing that normal services would be operating, and it was only after long waits at bus stops that they discovered that there would be no buses until 9 a.m. However, to cope with the expected influx of people into the city centres, it was decided that, 'Main line railways will be running a normal service today with extra late services to suburban stations.' In spite of the normal confusion prevailing at such times, the official comment on the situation was 'Everything going fine'.

The confusion was not helped by those who had either not yet heard that these two days were public holidays, or were unsure as to when the holiday started, and if it applied to them. In Widnes,

Workers went to work as usual this morning, only to be told on arrival that the holiday was in force. School children, likewise, put in an appearance, but they were sent home until Thursday morning.

They were not the only ones, as the *London Evening News* reported:

Hundreds of workers in the big West End shops jostled each other to-day – some on their way to work, others trying to get home after having reported for duty only to find doors locked. At every bus stop was a knot of people. Each one questioned gave the same answer. 'I thought the holiday started after three o'clock to-day, when Mr Churchill speaks.' Buses, running Sunday schedules, were packed to overflowing. No-one paid any heed to conductresses who called out as each batch tried to board their buses, 'If you're on your way to work you'll be coming back on the next trip.'

The *Liverpool Echo* reported that, 'Groups of girls who had come mistakenly to work stood outside the shops and factories or offices where they were employed, uncertain for a time, what they were to do – and then went home, rejoicing, but a little disconsolate that they had turned out at all.' The *Scotsman* noted, 'Considerable numbers of men and women proceeded as usual to their work yesterday morning, only to find the workshops closed down. Quickly the workers returned to their homes, and no doubt they were soon ready to take their part in the general rejoicing.'

The main line railway stations were busier than normal, being full of a mixture of people, some still trying to get to work, some having done so earlier and now, having been informed of their mistake, on their way home again, and some, aware of the holiday, making their way to city centres, or to friends or relatives, to celebrate.

In the suburbs, queues became the order of the day. With the holiday in mind there were queues outside shops selling fireworks. In Caernarvon, 'There was a last minute rush, especially among schoolchildren to buy up the remaining stocks of flags and bannerettes . . . shopping centres were thronged with people buying food, flags, newspapers and smokes.' There was a general shortage of cigarettes. In Bath, 'A number of tobacconists had run out of cigarettes by the middle of the morning, so heavy was the run on their stock.' There were queues, too, at bakers' shops for a two-day supply of bread. In St Helens, 'Today the principal occupation of the town was hanging bunting – and queuing up at the food shops.'

Bells, which back in 1940 were to be the signal of an invasion, now became the sound of victory. The bells of Chester Cathedral rang out their victory peal for an hour that morning. In Croydon a carillon of bells was lent by Gillett and Johnson, the local bell founders. In Liverpool, 'Victory chimes rang out in a grand crescendo over Liverpool today. They rang from churches and the municipal buildings.' In Didsbury, Edgar Buckle, the manager of the Capitol cinema, rang a half-hourly carillon throughout the day on the tubular organ-bells which he had taken out onto the balcony overlooking the street. In a similar vein the *Daily Sketch* reported:

> No public house, no village green and no buses. That is Walesby, a North Lincolnshire village of 27 people. But Walesby's two churches have 16 bells, and from early morning until well into the night the village men kept the bells going – playing hymn tunes and patriotic songs.

During the morning and early afternoon, many people went to church services; the *Manchester City News* reported that the day:

Medical students parading their mascot through central London. *(IWM HU92010)*

. . . had begun quietly enough with women and girls kneeling in the pews of St Ann's Church. At the Cathedral similar services were being conducted by the Bishop of Manchester, Dr Guy Warman, and at 11.30 the Lord Mayor, the Lady Mayoress, and the Town Clerk took their places among the congregation. Very quietly, some of the women were weeping.

At Westminster Abbey there were thanksgiving services every hour, while in Liverpool that morning there was an open-air service of thanksgiving for victory held outside the Royal Liver Building, which followed the traditional naval form of service. The large gathering there comprised mainly men and women of the naval services, with a sprinkling of civilians.

At Liverpool Cathedral, a special service had been planned for some time, to follow the announcement of victory by the Prime Minister. But from eight o'clock that morning large numbers of people began to arrive there, as at many other places of worship, to give thanks for peace. They soon reached such numbers that a Canon Residentiary, Canon C.F.H. Soulby, decided to conduct improvised services in which the crowds could all take part. The first was at ten o'clock, with a second, choral service, at eleven. Every seat was filled. The singing included 'Praise God From Whom All Blessings Flow', the national anthem, and 'Praise My Soul, The King of Heaven'.

Early in the morning, the flags of the Allied Nations, numbering about 40, were unfurled in the centre of the Cathedral, suspended from the galleries, and providing a fine splash of colour. A great many people placed slips, containing the names of their lost ones, in the Cenotaph in the War Memorial Transept, for remembrance.

In Colchester, Doreen Last remembered:

A group of school friends and I walked to town to see the Victory Processions going past the Town Hall and Main Street to attend St Peter's Church at the top of North Hill (where civic services always took place). Then we returned to watch them come out and continue back to the Town Hall where the Mayor spoke from the balcony, then gave us a timetable of events for the rest of the day.

At Chester Cathedral over 2,000 people packed the service of

Another crowd, this time outside Parliament. Big Ben shows 3.00 – the moment that the Prime Minister began his historic broadcast to the nation. *(IWM HU92005)*

Holborn. The Mayor gives a speech to the public from a balcony decorated with the flags of the Allies. Such local meetings, with speeches by local dignitaries, were features of many VE-Day celebrations.

thanksgiving, while in many of the towns and villages of North Wales, the day opened with united services of thanksgiving. In Edinburgh, all seats in the cathedral were occupied, while so many people crowded into St John's Church, Princes Street, for the eleven o'clock service, that it had to be relayed to an adjoining hall. Even then, many had to be turned away.

The Archbishop of Canterbury, who was Bishop of London throughout the Blitz, wrote a message to London:

I have been asked, as one who has been among them through blitz and bomb and rocket, to give a message to my fellow Londoners, which at this time of victory they can read in their own homes. Perhaps the old home has gone beyond repair, or still has its wartime patchings of roofs and ceilings and windows. But even so, London is our home again, with the peace and security of a home, free from the intrusions of droning engines of destruction, blast and sudden death – our own again. As we give thanks to God for all that this victory means for us and for the world, let us thank Him especially for our homes restored to us and all that they mean. Many must wait indeed till houses are built in their thousands; many must wait until sons and daughters, fathers and mothers come back from the war; and some will not return.

And we cannot forget the millions in Europe, dispossessed, scattered, hungry and homeless. But the grace of homeliness has returned to the earth, and to London. Let us thank God for that, and pray that our homes may be made all that they should be, not only houses well built, airy and clean, but homes where families dwell together in mutual trust, loyalty, affection and godliness.

As we look round on a London at peace we may adapt for our own use the words of the Psalmist: 'Walk about London, and go round about her: and tell the towers thereof, Mark well her bulwarks, set up her houses: that ye may tell them that come after. For this God is our God for ever and ever; He shall be our guide unto death – and beyond. High and low, rich and poor: one with another, Praise the Lord.'

At 10.00 that morning, after wireless communications with the German High Command in the still-occupied Channel Islands, the destroyers HMS *Bulldog* and *Beagle* left Plymouth for a pre-arranged rendezvous off Guernsey, arriving there at 2.00 p.m., to commence making arrangements for the surrender of the German garrison, numbering about 10,000 men.

The Bailiff of Guernsey told the States (Parliament):

The German Authorities have assured me that until such time as the Allies arrive in the Island, they will on their side do all that is necessary to ensure that the discipline of their troops will be maintained and that they will govern themselves in an orderly manner vis-a-vis the civilian population.

After 3 o'clock this afternoon all flags can be hoisted throughout the Island and I would suggest that further celebration should not take place until the arrival of the Allies. There is, however, no objection to Thanksgiving Services being held meanwhile.

## AFTERNOON

After a quiet start, the day began to liven up after lunchtime. In Edinburgh crowds began to gather outside the American Red Cross Service Club and the Register House, and soon extra police had to be brought in, the crowd had become so big. Thousands of people, mainly youngsters, had gathered outside, and from the balcony and windows, chewing gum and chocolate were showered upon them, followed by hats and, in typical American fashion, ticker-tape. A US Marine on the balcony led the community singing, including, 'Roll out the Barrel', 'The Yanks are Coming', 'Tipperary', and 'Land of Hope and Glory'. For those who did not want to take part in such public celebrations, or who liked horses, there was racing at Newmarket that afternoon, a full card of six races from 1.00 to 3.30, including the 1,000 Guineas at 2.30 (won by Sun Stream at 5-2).

In London, the first few holidaymakers began to arrive early on, easily distinguishable by the smatterings of red, white and blue. At first they toured the sights, but as their numbers grew they gradually assembled in the main spots. The *Liverpool Echo* reported, 'There were early indications that Buckingham Palace would be the no. 1 centre of attraction.' The *London Evening News* agreed:

At Buckingham Palace four women formed the first queue. They took their seats on the wall in front of the balcony. 'We had the time of our lives', said one of them. 'We lost the last train home, but that didn't matter so much, because we did not intend to go home anyway, as we wanted to be here first this morning.' A few people walked round the Victoria Memorial, while the inevitable American soldier talked to the inevitable policeman outside the Palace gates. In the Strand were market carts and horses . . . with red, white and blue trappings. A proud pony had a Union Jack draped on each side of the shafts. Many women wore national emblems, mostly red, white and blue rosettes. One had trimmed her hat with coloured ribbons.

This scene in Trafalgar Square, as the crowd listens to Churchill's speech, gives some impression of the vast gatherings in London and other cities that day. *(IWM HU92004)*

Whitehall soon became packed, although Downing Street itself was deserted, as the public were not allowed beyond the Whitehall entrance, where two police officers stood on duty. The crowd outside Buckingham Palace gradually grew to a multitude. Cheers broke out for the drums and fifes which accompanied the new guard along The Mall to St James's Palace, and for the smart Irish Guards band playing the old palace guard back to the Wellington Barracks. Both bands were followed by crowds of people, but that seemed to make no difference to size of the multitude standing outside the Palace itself.

Shortly after one o'clock the Prime Minister left Downing Street for lunch with the King and Queen at the Palace. As the open car drove slowly along, the growing crowd recognised the passenger in the black civilian suit, and closed in around it, cheering loudly, while the police, with great difficulty, kept a narrow passage open for it. 'Smiling and radiantly happy, Mr Churchill gave the V-sign time and time again to the crowd as he drove into the Palace.' It was the first time since the surrender that the Prime Minister and the King had met. The King wrote in his diary:

> We congratulated each other on the end of the European War. The day we have been longing for has arrived at last and we can look back with thankfulness to God that our tribulation is over.

Soon there were massive crowds in Piccadilly, Whitehall and the roads leading to the Palace, where the throng waited for the moment when the royal family would come out onto the balcony. The *Daily Sketch* estimated that at least 100,000 people were around the Victoria Memorial and in the precincts for most of the afternoon. The *London Evening News* also reported the scenes:

> At Downing Street, too, there were thousands of people. Some had waited all night in the hope of catching a glimpse of Mr Churchill. Londoners are standing now in great crowds stretching from Downing Street, past the Cenotaph to the entrance gates of Palace Yard. It is a very orderly and cheery crowd, and it is lining the pavement's edge and keeping clear of the entrance to Parliament. Chanting 'V for Victory' and cheering and singing lustily, a party of 200 students from King's College, in the Strand, paraded in the streets of the West End. Most of them wore gay red, white and blue favours. A number of them brandished flags of the Allied nations. They were the subject of numerous bantering remarks from the celebrating crowds. The students marched four abreast through the West End, and then returned to their college . . . There was an unofficial victory parade in Oxford Street by holidaymakers in improvised uniforms of red, white and blue under a canopy of waving flags. Some women paraders showed remarkable ingenuity in their attire, particularly in blouses fashioned out of flags. Music was provided by youths from London Polytechnic.

A bunch of girls, all wearing victory caps swung along the middle of the road, arm-in-arm, singing 'Tipperary'. Ice cream stalls and restaurants were busy, but most people ignored the [Belsen] horror camp newsreel, preferring to forget that side of the war – for today.

In Liverpool, the celebrations that afternoon featured a grand procession. All branches of the military services, civil defence organisations, and civilian workers assembled at Birkenhead Park main entrance and moved off at 2.15 p.m. along Conway Street and Argyle Street to reach Hamilton Square in time to hear Churchill's broadcast which was followed by a religious service conducted by Canon G.F. Smith.

Sheet music: 'When They Sound the Last All Clear'. By 1945 much popular music looked forward to the post-war period.

Everywhere, in the cities, towns and villages up and down the country, in public squares, in pubs, or in the peace of their own front rooms, people tuned in to the BBC to hear the historic broadcast of the Prime Minister's speech, in which the war in Europe would be officially declared over. The *Manchester City News* reported that:

. . . excitement mounted steadily until, at five minutes to three, the vast crowds made it impossible to get nearer to the Town Hall main entrance than Cross Street. The City Police Band swung from Rachmaninoff to a popular music-hall song, youths threw lighted rip-raps from the steps of the statues and the crowds applauded three RAF boys who had swarmed to the top of a lamp-post . . . At one minute to three, sailors were hauling their girls on to the roofs of air raid shelters and urchins clambered to the tops of lamp-posts to hear the Premier's announcement.

'All clear'. Soldiers, sailors, airmen and civilians swarm over a lorry to celebrate peace in Europe. *(IWM HU49571A)*

## 3.00 P.M.

At the stroke of three o'clock, the crowds hushed to listen to the familiar voice of Winston Churchill. President Truman, General de Gaulle and Marshal Stalin also gave speeches to their own people at about the same hour. For Russians Stalin's speech really did come as a surprise – there had been a complete media silence about the surrender – Moscow newspapers that morning still carried the slogan 'Death to the German invader'.

Winston Churchill broadcast to the nation from the War Cabinet Office at 10 Downing Street, the room from which Neville Chamberlain had made his own speech on 3 September 1939, announcing that, 'This country is at war with Germany.' Such was the importance of the speech that little was left to chance; Churchill's private room at the House of Commons was also wired up ready for him to give the speech from there should anything unforeseen occur. At last people heard the words they had awaited for so long.

Yesterday morning at 2.41 a.m. at headquarters, General Jodl, the representative of the German High Command and Grand Admiral Dönitz, the designated head of the German State, signed the act of unconditional surrender of all German land, sea, and air forces in Europe to the Allied Expeditionary Force, and simultaneously to the Soviet High Command.

General Bedell Smith, Chief of Staff of the Allied Expeditionary Force, and General François Sevez signed the document on behalf of the Supreme Commander of the Allied Expeditionary Force, and General Suslaparov signed on behalf of the Russian High Command.

Today this agreement will be ratified and confirmed at Berlin, where Air Chief Marshal Tedder, Deputy Supreme Commander of the Allied Expeditionary Force, and General de Lattre de Tassigny will sign on behalf of General Eisenhower. Marshal Zhukov will sign on behalf of the Soviet High Command. The German representatives will be Field Marshal Keitel, Chief of the High Command, and the Commanders-in-Chief of the German Army, Navy, and Air Force.

Hostilities will end officially at one minute after midnight tonight, but in the interests of saving lives the 'cease-fire' began yesterday to be sounded all along the front, and our dear Channel Islands are also to be freed today.

The Germans are still in places resisting the Russian troops, but should they continue to do so after midnight they will, of course, deprive themselves of the protection of the laws of war, and will be attacked from all quarters by the Allied troops. It is not surprising that on such long fronts and in the existing disorder of the enemy the commands of the German High Command should not in every case be obeyed immediately. This does not, in our opinion, with the best military advice at our disposal, constitute any reason for withholding from the nation the facts communicated to us by General Eisenhower of the unconditional surrender already signed at Rheims, nor should it prevent us from celebrating today and tomorrow as Victory in Europe days.

Today, perhaps, we shall think mostly of ourselves. Tomorrow we shall pay a particular tribute to our Russian comrades, whose prowess in the field has been one of the grand contributions to the general victory.

The German war is therefore at an end. After years of intense preparation, Germany hurled herself on Poland at the beginning of September 1939; and in pursuance of our guarantee to Poland and in agreement with the French Republic, Great Britain, the British Empire and Commonwealth of Nations, declared war upon this foul aggression. After gallant France had been struck down we, from this island and from our united Empire, maintained the struggle single-handed for a whole year until we were joined by the military might of Soviet Russia and later by the overwhelming power and resources of the United States of America.

Finally almost the whole world has combined against the evil-doers, who are now prostrate before us. Our gratitude to our splendid Allies goes forth from all our hearts in this island and throughout the British Empire.

We may allow ourselves a brief period of rejoicing; but let us not forget for a moment the toil and efforts that lie ahead. Japan, with all her treachery and greed, remains unsubdued. The injury she has inflicted on Great Britain, the United States, and other countries, and her detestable cruelties, call for justice and retribution. We must now devote all our strength and resources to the completion of our task, both at home and abroad. Advance Britannia! Long live the cause of freedom! God Save the King!

Peter Baker remembered, 'At 3 p.m. the Prime Minister gave his never to be forgotten broadcast to the nation, a very moving experience.' In many places loudspeakers relayed the speech to the crowds, including 60,000 in Trafalgar Square. In Bath, 'The Prime Minister's broadcast was relayed during a break in the programme at the Beau Nash cinema this afternoon, and the King's speech will similarly be heard by the audience at 9 p.m. Police permission has been obtained for an extension loudspeaker to be fixed outside the cinema so that speeches may be heard by people in the street.'

In Croydon:

> Over loudspeakers from the Town Hall, at three o'clock, was broadcast the strong, emotional voice of the Prime Minister announcing the unconditional surrender of the German armed forces and the sounding of the cease-fire throughout Europe. The bells had been rung and a programme of music was broadcast, which included many popular songs in the singing of which thousands joined . . . After a brief silence the Mayor led the crowds in a short service of thanksgiving, reading the prayer specially composed for VE-Day and leading the singing of two hymns.

There were similar scenes in Lancashire:

> At Crosby to-day, after the Prime Minister's speech, relayed throughout the borough from the Central School, the Mayor (Alderman H. Preston Reynolds) addressed the crowds in the streets from the roof of the building and music was relayed.

In Jersey the Bailiff addressed crowds outside the Royal Court building, introducing the public relay of Winston Churchill's speech, at the end of which the Bailiff announced that this was an appropriate moment for the 'raising of flags'. (Actually the German commander, Vice-Admiral Friedrich Hüffmeier, did not capitulate until the following day, when the first British troops landed, while Alderney was not liberated until the 16th.)

After Churchill's announcement, in Manchester's Albert Square, war reserve policemen unfurled each of the forty-four flags of the United Nations, beginning with the Union flag, while in Folkestone, in a reflection of the popular song, the last 'all clear,' was sounded. During the war the sirens there had sounded 4,165 air raid warnings and 102 shell warnings.

# CHAPTER 5

# *VE-Day*

## A NIGHT OF REJOICING

Outside Buckingham Palace, at the close of Churchill's broadcast, the crowd was lifted even higher by the appearance on the balcony, for the first of many times that day, of the royal family. While they stood waving to the crowd a Mosquito came droning down Pall Mall at less than 1,000 feet and passed over the Royal Standard flying from the palace roof. The *Daily Sketch* commented:

> How they cheered the King in his uniform of Admiral of the Fleet, the Queen in turquoise, Princess Elizabeth in her A.T.S. [Auxiliary Territorial Service, the women's branch of the Army] uniform and Princess Margaret in powder blue when they made their appearances throughout the afternoon and evening on the Palace balcony.

Joyce West also remembered:

> My father took me, aged ten, to Trafalgar Square, and then on to Buckingham Palace on VE-Day. We saw the royal family come on to the balcony. The cheering and noise were very exciting, and I thought it would go on for ever.

After his speech Churchill was driven from Downing Street to the House of Commons, riding on the hood of his open car, for which mounted police had to force a way through the immense cheering crowd which had gathered in Whitehall. He received a further tumultuous reception from the packed House. At 3.15 the Prime Minister formally announced the end of the European war to the House, repeating the contents of his broadcast:

> I have only two or three sentences to add. They will convey to the House my deep gratitude to this House of Commons, which has proved itself the strongest foundation for waging war that has ever been seen in the whole of our long history . . . We have all of us made mistakes, but the strength

Churchill, just visible left of centre, as he makes his way to the Houses of Parliament after making his victory broadcast. *(IWM HU86188)*

of the Parliamentary institutions has been shown to enable it at the same moment to preserve all the title-deeds of democracy while waging war in the most stern and protracted form . . . I beg to move that this house do now attend the Church of St Margaret, Westminster, to give humble and reverent thanks to Almighty God for our deliverance from the threat of German domination.

This was the identical resolution moved at the time of the 1918 armistice, delivered by a prime minister with a keen sense of history. Then, the Serjeant-at-Arms, carrying the mace, led the procession with the Speaker at its head, followed by Privy Councillors, then junior ministers and the rank-and-file MPs, walking four abreast, across Old Palace Yard to the church. After the service, which lasted about twenty minutes, the procession returned to the House of Commons. In the House of Lords, Lord Woolton read the same statement on the surrender, after which the peers, headed by

The Prime Minister giving his famous V-sign to the crowds outside the Ministry of Health. *(IWM H41849)*

the Lord Chancellor, adjourned to their own service of thanksgiving in Westminster Abbey.

At 4.15 p.m. the doors of the palace balcony opened again, and the earlier scene was repeated. It happened once more at 5.30. But this time there was a difference. Between the King and Queen appeared Churchill, bare-headed, and in sombre clothes. A great shout went up: 'Churchill!'

The early edition of the *Evening News* had announced:

> Mr Churchill intends to show himself to the victory crowds – probably at about five o'clock – on the balcony of the Ministry of Health, near the Houses of Parliament. People who want to see the Prime Minister may expect to do so in Parliament Street, then – and he may be persuaded, too, to say a few words into microphones for the throng. Mr Churchill will probably have members of the Cabinet and Service chiefs with him. The balcony has been specially decorated with Union Jacks and above it today float as centrepieces of a wonderful display all the Allied flags, the Union Jack, the Red Flag with the Hammer and Sickle in gold, and the Stars and Stripes. Crowning all, flying from a flag-staff over the building, was the Union Jack again.

There was a huge crowd outside the ministry when, shortly before 6 p.m., the Prime Minister stepped out onto the flag-draped balcony, accompanied by members of the War Cabinet. A massive roar went up in greeting and when, in response, he gave his famous V-sign and beamed, the roar of enthusiasm became even louder. His first words were 'God bless you all. This is your victory', and the crowd roared back, 'and yours'. Churchill went on:

In all our long history we have never seen a greater day than this. Everyone, man or woman, has done their share. No one has flinched. Neither long years nor the fierce attacks of the enemy have in any way, weakened the unbending resolve of the British nation. God bless you all.

He turned to go, but the crowd were almost hysterical, he faced round to them once more and waved his hat repeatedly. Then Ernest Bevin stepped forward and called out, 'Three cheers for Victory.' The crowd duly responded, and the cabinet ministers joined in.

Elsewhere the party was beginning to warm up; bands were playing, marches and processions taking place, locally a few street parties were going on, although the majority of those would take place in the following days. In Liverpool, two hours after the Prime Minister's broadcast, the Mayor read a

The Ministry of Health building in Whitehall (*left*). Churchill can be seen in the centre of the central balcony, just over the main entrance, from where he spoke to the massive crowd. *(IWM AP12359F)*

These three adverts from the *London Evening News* of 8 May show some of the many facets of the day itself – thanksgiving, celebration, and looking towards the future.

proclamation from the town hall, which was relayed by loud-speakers at the junctions of Oriel Road–Trinity Road, Merton Road–Oriel Road, Hawthorne Road–Linacre Lane, in Litherland Road, and at the Canal Bridge. A city council meeting in Birmingham, fixed for that afternoon, soon had to be abandoned when it was found to be impossible to form a quorum, and large crowds in the city's Victoria Square, led by the Lord Mayor, sang patriotic songs for hours on end.

A crowd of schoolchildren set the rejoicing going in St Helens with an unofficial procession headed by 'Lord Haw Haw', as chief guide. A collection, taken to provide the bonfire material, indicated the public enthusiasm to see him 'well fixed'.

And in Bath, 'From morn till night great crowds were everywhere watching impromptu fancy-dress processions, taking part in impromptu singing . . . Streets were packed.'

There were sports. In Liverpool, 'Those who want to wind up today's celebrations with a football match have two to choose from.' At Goodison Park there was the final of the H.D. Hughes Cup for service sides, between RAF and Fleet Air Arm teams starting at 7.00 p.m. As was often the case during the war, both service teams were composed almost entirely of league players. The second match was the West Lancashire ATC final between Waterloo Grammar School and Prescot, at Anfield, kicking off at 7.15 p.m.

## 9.00 P.M.

The next formal item on that day's agenda was the King's speech, due for nine o'clock. In Greenwich, as in so many other places, 'A rapidly growing crowd was assembling to hear the Royal speech, relayed to them from the [Borough] hall.' Just before the King broadcast on the wireless, a woman described as 'a mother of Britain' spoke, and revealed that she had 'given her son to the cause of victory'. This mother was in fact Mrs Mabel Henderson, the wife of a retired civil servant, who had been awarded the British Empire Medal for her work with the Women's Voluntary Service (WVS). Then, at nine o'clock, the King spoke. His voice was by now familiar to just about everyone, because of his annual broadcasts to the nation every Christmas Day since 1939.

> Today we give thanks to Almighty God for a great deliverance. Speaking from our Empire's oldest capital city, war-battered but never for one moment daunted or dismayed – speaking from London, I ask you to join with me in that act of thanksgiving.
>
> Germany, the enemy who drove all Europe into war, has been finally overcome. In the Far East we have yet to deal with the Japanese, a determined and cruel foe. To this we shall turn with the utmost resolve and with all our resources. But at this hour, when the dreadful shadow of war has passed from our hearths and homes in these islands, we may at last make one pause for thanksgiving and then turn our thoughts to the tasks all over the world which peace in Europe brings with it.
>
> First, let us remember those who will not come back, their constancy and courage in battle, their sacrifice and endurance in the face of a merciless enemy: let us remember the men in all the Services and the women in all the Services who have laid down their lives. We have come to

the end of our tribulation, and they are not with us at the moment of our rejoicing.

Next let us salute in proud gratitude the great host of the living who have brought us to victory. I cannot praise them to the measure of each one's service, for in a total war the efforts of all rise to the same noble height and all are devoted to the common purpose. Armed or unarmed, men and women, you have fought, striven, and endured to your utmost No one knows that better than I do; and as your King I thank with a full heart those who bore arms so valiantly on land and sea, or in the air; and all civilians who, shouldering their many burdens, have carried them unflinchingly without complaint.

With those memories in our minds, let us think what it was that has upheld us through nearly six years of suffering and peril. The knowledge that everything was at stake: our freedom, our independence, our very existence as a people; but the knowledge also that in defending ourselves we were defending the liberties of the whole world; that our cause was the cause not of this nation only, not of this Empire and Commonwealth only, but of every land where freedom is cherished and law and liberty go hand in hand. In the darkest hours we knew that the enslaved and isolated peoples of Europe looked to us; their hopes were our hopes; their confidence confirmed our faith. We knew that, if we failed, the last remaining barrier against a world-wide tyranny would have fallen in ruins. But we did not fail. We kept our faith with ourselves and with one another; we kept faith and unity with our great allies. That faith and unity have carried us to victory through dangers which at times seemed overwhelming.

So let us resolve to bring to the tasks which lie ahead the same high confidence in our mission. Much hard work awaits us, both in the restoration of our own country after the ravages of war and in helping to restore peace and sanity to a shattered world.

This comes upon us at a time when we have given of our best. For five long years and more, heart and brain, nerve and muscle have been directed upon the overthrow of Nazi tyranny. Now we turn, fortified by success, to deal with our last remaining foe. The Queen and I know the ordeals which you have endured throughout the Commonwealth and Empire. We are proud to have shared some of these ordeals with you, and we know also that together we shall all face the future with stern resolve and prove that our reserves of will-power and vitality are inexhaustible.

There is great comfort in the thought that the years of darkness and danger in which the children of our country have grown up are over and, please God, for ever. We shall have failed, and the blood of our dearest will have flowed in vain, if the victory which they died to win does not lead to a lasting peace, founded on justice and established in good will. To that, then, let us turn our thoughts on this day of just triumph and proud sorrow; and then take up our work again, resolved as a people to do nothing unworthy of those who died for us and to make the world such a world as they would have desired, for their children and for ours.

This is the task to which now honour binds us. In the hour of danger we humbly committed our cause into the Hand of God, and He has been our Strength and our Shield. Let us thank Him for His mercies, and in this hour of Victory commit ourselves and our new task to the guidance of that same strong Hand.

The speech lasted just under a quarter of an hour, at the end of which the crowds assembled up and down the country sang the national anthem. Then, the King and Queen, who had now changed into a white evening dress and wore a diamond tiara, and the princesses came out on to the palace balcony once again. By now, the police estimated that the crowd outside the palace alone was 100,000 strong.

At 10.30 the Houses of Parliament were floodlit, and Churchill, now dressed in his trademark siren suit, returned to the Ministry of Health balcony where he conducted the crowd in 'Land of Hope and Glory'. After that he gave another short speech. 'A terrible foe has been cast down, and awaits our judgement and our mercy.' He then spoke about the future:

After that we must begin the task of rebuilding our homes, and must turn ourselves to fulfil our duty to our own countrymen, to our gallant Allies the United States who were so foully and treacherously attacked by Japan. We will go hand-in-hand with them, and even if it is a hard struggle, we shall not be the ones who fail. We were the first to draw the sword against tyranny. After a while we stood alone. Did anybody want to give in?

After the Prime Minister's speech, the crowds outside Buckingham Palace were rewarded for their patience when the King, Queen and the two princesses appeared on the balcony. This shot shows the crowd outside waving as the royal family make the first of several appearances that day. *(IWM HU92009)*

The crowd roared 'No'. 'Were we downhearted?' – another 'No'.

> So we came back after long months from the jaws of death, out of the mouth of hell, while all the world wondered.

He then gave them a victory sign and, to a tremendous roar, left the balcony. Then he returned to Downing Street and to work.

At about 10.45 the royal family all came out on to the balcony once again and stayed for about ten minutes. Shortly after 11.00 the princesses slipped out. Speaking in 1985, the Queen recalled:

> I remember the thrill and relief after the previous day's waiting for the Prime Minister's announcement of the end of the war in Europe. My parents went out on the balcony in response to the huge crowds outside.

I think we went on the balcony every hour, six times, and then when the excitement of the floodlights being switched on got through to us, my sister and I realised we couldn't see what the crowds were enjoying. My mother had put on her tiara for the occasion, so we asked my parents if we could go out and see for ourselves. I remember we were terrified of being recognised, so I pulled my uniform cap well down over my eyes. A Grenadier officer amongst our party of sixteen people said he refused to be seen in the company of another officer improperly dressed, so I had to put my cap on normally. We cheered the King and Queen on the balcony and then walked through the streets. I remember a line of unknown people linking arms and walking down Whitehall, all of us just swept along on a tide of happiness and relief. I remember the amazement of my cousin, just back from four and a half years in a prisoner of war camp, walking freely with his family in the friendly throng. And I also remember when someone exchanged hats with a Dutch sailor, the poor man coming along with us in order to get his cap back. After crossing Green Park we stood outside and shouted 'We want the King', and were successful in seeing my parents on the balcony, having cheated slightly because we sent a message into the house to say we were waiting outside. I think it was one of the most memorable nights of my life.

Stevie Smith also described the scenes:

The Union Jack and the Stars and Stripes and every bit of red, white and blue was off the market by this time, beer was no longer to be had in the public bars, but there were still a few drips of Scotch in the private bottle . . . The people came out rather shyly at first, they stood about in stiff party-mannered groups . . . they were like good children at a party, just before the thing got really going, it was that moment the hostess dreads . . . The pause, that frightful hostess-nightmare, lasted not five minutes of Big Ben's time. In the elegant avenues of South Kensington, from the polyglot centre of Piccadilly Circus, in Lambeth and its Walk, in Seven Sisters Road and the Elephant and Castle, in Stepney, Houndsditch and Mildmay Park, in the remote suburbs of Parson's Green and Purley, on the Heath that is Hampstead and the Common that is Tooting, the people began to dance and laugh.

Roy Wilcox also remembered:

> Some of my friends were in the Boys' Brigade and were giving a display at
> the Pump Room in Bath that evening. A number of us went there to see
> the display. After we left the Pump Room we joined the crowds that had
> gathered at the Abbey Churchyard and outside the Guildhall, Bath. Being
> 13 years old we could not stay long and had to be at home at a reasonable
> time. It was still light as Double British Summer Time was in being.

Concerts and dances were the next entertainment in many places. Local
bands toured their areas, like Salvation Army bands at Christmas. In other
places music was piped into the streets, using the public address systems set
up for the Prime Minister's and King's speeches. In Liverpool:

> Singing and dancing will follow until midnight in the Town Hall and in
> Derby Park. The music will be relayed from the Town Hall to the park, and
> this part of the programme will be repeated on VE plus 1 day . . . Flags and
> bunting adorn the square in front of Hoylake Post Office where open-air
> dancing will take place to-night and to-morrow night . . . At Denbigh there
> will be a dance in the Town Hall to-night and also dancing in the streets.

In Birmingham the Lord Mayor said:

> I was impressed, too, by the way in which the children had contrived to
> get bands. I don't know whether the Salvage Department will agree –
> I hope they will – but the children made impressive use of dustbin lids.
> I only hope, now that V-days are over, that the children will be good
> enough to return the lids to the right bins.

The *Kentish Mercury* reported that:

> Amazing scenes were witnessed at the Marquis of Granby junction of New
> Cross Road and Lewisham Way. A carnival dance at the Palais de Danse
> was full to overflowing, but those who could not obtain admission were
> not denied the pleasure of the great occasion. The music from the ballroom
> was relayed to them in the street below, and there, at midnight, a company
> estimated by the police to number about two thousand was revelling in all
> the frenzied enjoyment of the moment.

One of the most immediate dividends of peace was the end of the black-out, in force since the beginning of the war. For children, the sight of switched-on street lights was a VE spectacle all in itself. Many could not remember what they looked like. *(Lewisham Local Archives)*

In Glasgow, 'They danced jigs and eightsomes in front of the City Chambers, performed sweeping wonders with the palais glide and wound up in long serpentine columns, singing and laughing in happy eddies round the staider islands of civilian sightseers.' The *Western Daily Press* reported that, 'The Americans, naturally, were at the front in any fun that was going.'

With darkness came the bonfires. For days children had been collecting whatever they could to put on the fire. Ken Moore remembered:

I was about eleven when the war ended. There were parties in most streets. Pointed paper hats, flags on the houses. A line of small flags is draped across the road. Our gang have hacksaws and choppers, and school macs on. The gang from Lankstone Road are with us. Opposite the Prince of Wales pub, on the edge of the tip, there is a tree; it's two feet across, we start chopping, hacking – 'It's going! Oooh! There's a copper coming.' It crashes down, landing with its ends touching the copper's bike. We run. The others run towards Daisy Farm Park. Three of us scatter down the bank, then rush up a ramp, by the top we are out of puff. We come out on

West Croydon. One of the many thousands of bonfires which lit the sky that night. *(IWM HU87439)*

Prince of Wales Lane, round a hedge: 'Got yah' – it's John Dent, the local copper. I think 'Cor! Wait till my dad finds out.' He takes us back to the felled tree, and makes us cut it up. It takes six of us to roll it up to our party in Daisy Farm Road. We add it to the fire . . .

We are in a long train, hands on hips, doing the conga, going down the middle of the road, I'm at the head, singing 'Eye-eye-conga!' We pass the YMCA, everyone shouts 'Hello!', we pass Molly Flint's shop, again 'Hello!' Our train goes on, into Yardley Wood bus garage, 'Eye-eye-conga', we are spotted; they make us go out of the main door of the garage.

Next day two of us sit on the gutter blowing the ashes to rekindle the fire. I remember having a black face.

Some police were not so understanding. In Glasgow the police reported that, 'Quite a number of youthful people have been arrested on charges of the theft of wood and other materials to feed the fires. In the Townhead district the crowd resented the intervention of two police officers and attacked them.'

All sorts of things went on the bonfires. Doreen Last recalled, 'We returned to Abbey Fields to enjoy many bonfires and the burning of all the mattresses and bunk beds from the air raid shelters.' Brian Martin remembered that, 'We burnt our gas masks on a fire in the garden.' With this kind of behaviour in mind, the Emergency Committee of Bristol City Council issued a notice, 'Gas masks are GOVERNMENT property and the public are asked to take care of these articles, avoiding wilful damage or destruction until further instructions can be issued as to their disposal.' Peter Baker was at RNAS Yeovilton, 'From all corners of the station literally dozens of sailors appeared carrying wooden-framed window black-outs, the destination being the middle of the parade square.' Not only rubbish went on the fires; in the hunt for fuel a lot of material meant for desperately-needed building repair was also grabbed, even the wooden wheelbarrows and other tools.

Brian Henderson remembered their bonfire:

We lived in a police cottage in a 1930s council housing estate in Hall Green, near the city boundary with Solihull. At the end of the war, I was eight. Our dad was a police constable, and mother was then an assistant manageress at a cake shop.

Our house was one of a block of four police houses, with other policemen living nearby in private housing. These men, with other neighbours, made a large bonfire on a grass reservation at the corner of our road. Less than a hundred yards away, in Sleaford Grove, the residents had their own bonfire in the centre of the highway. Some pieces of wooden furniture were among the fuel.

My enjoyment of the fire was short lived. One of the men kindly gave me a baked potato which had been cooked in the hot embers. As I took my first bite the hot potato skinned the roof of my mouth, so I ran home to my mum and spent a couple of uncomfortable days.

In numerous places the bonfires were part of the official celebrations; at St Helens, for example, 'A bonfire ring has been prepared round the town for this evening', or in a less urban setting, 'When darkness falls it is expected that the Welsh mountains will be ringed with beacon fires.' While in Croydon, 'In many parts of the town there were bonfires, not always authorised, and at Balfour Road, South Norwood, a life-size effigy of Hitler was burned.' Such effigies were a common, almost necessary part to any local bonfire. The *Bath Chronicle* reported how frequent such a thing was, 'Bath celebrated VE-Day . . . watching effigies of Hitler consumed by flames in a score and more parts of the city.' In Liverpool, 'Down another street in the city was a man carrying an effigy of Hitler, doomed, no doubt, to some form of ignominious destruction.'

Peter Baker's naval party soon developed:

We arrived in the NAAFI to find the black-out bonfire well alight, with what seemed like the whole of the station's sailors and wrens dancing around the fire singing, jitterbugging, doing the hokey-cokey, often falling over in the general excitement. Suddenly, on the outskirts of the parade ground in the direction of the gymnasium came the distinct sound of a thunderflash exploding, followed by several more explosions. After a lull in the proceedings the night sky was lit up by the discharge of a Very light. Obviously someone had managed to obtain, illicitly, a pistol and cartridges; soon the sky was ablaze with colour, red, green, blue, white and yellow. From across the road in the wardroom the officers could be heard singing, and there were more flares from that direction.

Not everyone liked the bonfires, or the accompanying fireworks. Joan Letts, 'I also remember celebrating VE-Day with a bonfire and fireworks by our local lake on Bixley Heath, although some people didn't agree with celebrating VE-Day when we were still at war with Japan. I couldn't remember watching peaceful fireworks and didn't like the bangs.'

For some, the sight was just too reminiscent of recent, more tragic events. In *Westminster at War*, William Sansom wrote:

> The watcher, more silent on his tower, would have then seen to grow with the vanishing day a strange and terrible mirage – for it seemed that in this hour of the end of almost six years there was imposed upon London a mirage of the days of bombardment. London, in a hundred places, was on fire again, the ghost of the Blitz was abroad . . . The ghosts of wardens and fire-guards and firemen were felt scurrying again down in the redness. Fireworks peppered the air with a parody of gunfire. The smell of burning wood charred the nostrils. And, gruesomely correct, some of the new street lights and fluorescent window lights in different parts glowed fiercely bluish-white, bringing again the shrill memory of the old white thermite glare of the bursting incendiary.

But, as the *Kentish Mercury* pointed out, 'The illusion, although accentuated by the crack of rockets, was nullified by the merry chatter and delirious singing of thousands of people.'

As with any bonfire night, the fire service was busy, 'Bootle NFS were called out to-day to Molyneux's premises in Chapel Street, where the debris prepared in readiness for a VE night bonfire had been set alight by children, and had to be extinguished by the firemen.'

For many, one of the spectacles of the day was the floodlighting of prominent buildings. After almost six years of black-out, it was another clear sign that the European war was over. In Croydon, 'Perhaps the climax of the celebrations was the appearance in North End towards midnight of pink and yellow neon lamps, which floodlit a great statue of Peace over Kennard's Stores before which thousands of people danced.' The *Bath Chronicle* reported, 'It was surprising how many people in the Abbey Church Yard were just content to stare at the floodlit west door of the Abbey, a sight which they had been deprived of for five years and eight months.'

Dancing in the street near Berkeley Square, London. *(IWM EA65885)*

Sybil Morley remembered:

> I had not been well and was away on holiday with my mother at Morecambe; I was very disappointed not to have been at home as it sounded as if my father and sister were having a wonderful time of celebration with the Americans. I can't really remember my mother and I doing anything special except looking at all the lights which were switched on at the seaside resort. No more black-out!

Arnold Beardwell recalled:

> My sister and I went to stay with our auntie in Earl's Court Gardens in London, and our aunt took us to the celebrations. I seem to remember us walking from my aunt's flat in Earl's Court to Kensington High Street – it was very crowded with very happy people. I especially recall the shop and street lights being on – what a change after the black-out.

As the evening wore on the celebrations grew warmer. The *Bath Chronicle* reported, 'Self-consciousness and reserve vanished on VE-Night. People of all classes mingled in common rejoicing. The officialdom of our always helpful policemen was at a minimum.' The *Liverpool Echo* reported a breakdown in social niceties, 'Our correspondent saw an epidemic of hand-shaking, even by people who had never seen each other before.' In Birmingham, 'Belisha beacons in the Square became footballs, everybody was dancing or marching about with arms linked right across the road. "We won't go home till morning", they sang. And they didn't.'

Of course there were some people who got drunk. Doreen Last remembered, 'Father took us to the Town Hall, outside of which were packed jovial people, to hear the Mayor's speech; but as the buses arrived they were attacked and had all their windows smashed. I think it was just due to over-excitement and exuberance; no doubt some of the crowd had been drinking.' Peter Baker also recalled lively scenes:

> During the partying several cadets managed, with the connivance of the sailors, to obtain a few glasses of beer, Although we had been told to return to our quarters by 10 p.m. none of us left the celebrations 'till long past midnight, although the party was still in progress with many very inebriated with the singing and dancing looking likely to go on all night. Our Officer in Charge returned to his bunk in the very early hours in quite a state of merriment; he didn't look very well next morning.

But few were really drunk; there just was not that much drink to be had. 'There will be no late closing of public houses tonight. Only one licensee had applied for an extension, and because the two magistrates on the bench were unable to agree the application failed. At Ruthin the public-houses are to remain open until 11 to-night.' The *Scotsman* reported, 'Questions as to the propriety of the suggestion that public bars should remain open a little longer than usual did not arise. The large majority of the places of public entertainments in Edinburgh closed last night between 7 and 8 o'clock because of the exhaustion of their supplies.'

Muriel Jones also remembered that evening, 'I was in the Walworth Road, and all the pubs emptied, and everyone was in the street, singing and dancing, everybody joined in – you danced with anybody. As you came

"He SAID he'd do it when the war was over—and I've got his thick pyjamas and hot water bottle ready for when he's finished."

Many people had made themselves or others promises as to what they would do when the great day finally arrived: a cartoon by Lee from the *London Evening News*.

through the streets they were burning bonfires, in the road.' Doreen Last recalled 'We didn't get home to my mother and little sister until midnight.'

A *Manchester City News* reporter wrote movingly of the end of a grand day:

As I pushed my way deeper into the Albert Square crowd – poop – a toy trumpet whisked past my ear, a flimsy streamer wrapped itself round my coat sleeve and I paused to allow right of way to a chain of conga-mongers. I took a look at the Town Hall clock. It was getting very close to midnight.

More people streamed into the square. There was no longer any room to dance on the shelter tops but the music still played, and they still danced below. More streamers – more noise. A pin-wheel screamed its way into the stately monument of Abel Heywood and ricocheted into nowhere.

VE-Day crowds in Piccadilly Circus. The unusual structure, put up to protect the plinth of the statue of Eros from German bombs, now makes a strange sort of statue itself, adorned with tiers of celebrating people. And, as the cartoon opposite shows, it had become a well-known landmark in the city. *(IWM EA65879)*

A rocket soared skywards and burst into a hundred tiny starlets. Three minutes to twelve!

All eyes gazed upwards towards the Town Hall clock. I stared too. It resembled a massive ghost towering skywards – eerie yet inspiring in the glow of the dazzling floodlighting. The singing stopped. No fireworks crackled, and everywhere was still as the two illuminated Union Jacks fluttered majestically at either side of the tower.

Then came zero hour, and the clock soberly boomed forth its twelve mighty strokes. With it came a deep sense of relief – this time it was really over.

Following the final stroke, the national anthem echoed through the square, and every one of those many thousands came proudly and impressively to attention.

In London, the King and Queen came out on to the balcony one last time just before 12.30. A few minutes later the floodlights were switched off and the crowd gradually began to disperse.

In Bath, the *Chronicle* recorded that:

At the bottom of Milsom street . . . hundreds of people sang in the roadway watching the six flaming torches on the Bath Gas Company's building. As midnight struck, the torches flickered and went out leaving only the traffic lights for illumination. A sudden hush descended on the concourse, then someone started singing 'Land of Hope and Glory'. It was taken up by everyone and standing there in the roadway and on the pavements they sang Arthur Benson's verses which expressed so well their hopes and faith in the future.

In Glasgow the evening finished for most of the crowd when the lights of George Square were turned off at 1.30. In Croydon it was 2.00 before 'the rejoicings' were stilled. In Guernsey, the *Weekly Press* reported that, 'Quite a number of islanders did not return to their homes on Tuesday evening. They chose, rather, to stay near the White Rock to ensure not missing anything. It was obvious soon after midnight that there were some ships outside.' Jenny D'Eath remembered that, in Norfolk, 'They were singing all night in the street.'

# CHAPTER 6

# *Later Victory Celebrations*

In Germany, British troops had the normal 6.30 reveille, followed by the usual sausage breakfast one hour later. However, each man got a pint of beer with dinner. Church bells rang to proclaim the peace, and church services were held across the country. As with their civilian counterparts back home, every soldier able to get to a radio listened to the Prime Minister's speech. The *Western Daily Press* quoted one soldier: 'Here in Germany surrounded by glum-faced civilians it was hard to realise it was a day of rejoicing, but our lads managed to celebrate.' Reuters' correspondent with the British Second Army wrote:

> VE-Day was celebrated by over 100,000 British troops in Germany with bonfires, Very lights of a dozen colours, and festivities in every mess and billet from the Weser to the Rhine, from the Rhine to the Elbe, and from the Baltic to Brussels. Lights blazed from unshuttered windows and headlights were dazzling.

Liberated prisoner of war Leslie Kerridge was still in Russian-occupied Germany. 'On the day of the surrender of Germany there were large scale celebrations in the Russian zone. The Russians were going slightly mad, getting thoroughly drunk and firing off everything from anti-aircraft guns to rifles. We had a very good time that day as the Russians were extra specially friendly.'

General Simpson, commander of the US Ninth Army, spent VE-Day with his Russian opposite number, Colonel-General Svetaiev at Zerbst, in the Russian sector. The *Daily Herald* reported:

> Highlight of the official rejoicings came when, at a concert in Zerbst town hall, which followed Svetaiev's lunch with Simpson, the American General was twice tossed high into the air and caught again in the stalwart arms of Russian soldiers. The lunch took place at a table about as long as a cricket

pitch, in a requisitioned German villa . . . there was every sort of toast, the most frequent being to Roosevelt, Stalin and Churchill. Very few Russians seem to have heard of President Truman.

In Cairo, British and other Allied troops celebrated the news of Germany's surrender by dancing through the street of the capital with equally jubilant Egyptians, while, more officially, a one hundred gun salute was fired.

British paratroopers find a warm welcome in Copenhagen. *(IWM BU5357)*

In Australia, VE-Day celebrations were muted, it being emphasised that for Australian forces there still remained the task of defeating the Japanese, a task far closer to home for them. However, in New Zealand, great crowds thronged the government buildings in Wellington, to celebrate the coming return of the victorious 2nd Division from Italy.

In Paris sirens and artillery salvos heralded peace. Crowds paraded the boulevards singing 'Tipperary' and the 'Marseillaise', with the biggest crowd assembling at the Arc de Triomphe. Loudspeakers in the Place de l'Opéra broadcast patriotic music, while at the thanksgiving service in Notre Dame Cathedral, the lesson was read by the British Ambassador, Duff Cooper. In Athens the end of the European war was greeted by sirens, bells, and volleys from rifles and pistols.

In Copenhagen the celebrations were especially warm, coming as they did just three days after the city's liberation. The *Liverpool Echo* reported that, 'People stormed newstands and fought for papers. Britons and Americans sought to escape as people kissed them and hoisted them onto their shoulders.' The previous day troops of the British 6th Airborne Division had landed in the country, to be joined later in the day by armoured cars of the Royal Dragoons, and elements of both groups paraded through the streets of the capital on VE-Day, to the cheers of the Danes.

In Oslo patriots freed from prison were carried shoulder high through the streets.

In Moscow's Red Square tens of thousands gathered to sing and dance, while victory demonstrations were staged outside the Allied embassies, and in Leningrad there was a parade of Red Army units.

Even in neutral Lisbon, large crowds marched down the main streets cheering, and chanting the names of the Allied leaders. Many people came together outside the British and US embassies, waving Allied flags and making V-signs, while in country districts shop windows displaying German propaganda were smashed.

## WEDNESDAY 9 MAY

Tomorrow for you, Far East, to-night is ours. *Stevie Smith*

That day's papers carried the news that Hermann Göring and Field Marshal Albert Kesselring had been captured by US troops in Austria.

The Channel Islands were waiting to be liberated. The *Guernsey Weekly Press* reported:

When dawn broke . . . people who had been eagerly and anxiously waiting perceived the dull, grey outline of two ships of the Royal Navy lying at anchor just off White Rock. Mr Churchill had kept his word. On Tuesday

Like many children all over the continent, these two little Belgian girls are dressed in the flags of Britain and the USA for the peace celebrations in Brussels. *(IWM BU5631)*

The children of Stoughton Infants' School, Guildford, and their teachers, make their own V-for-Victory sign. *(Courtesy of Froglets Publications)*

afternoon he had said 'Our dear Channel Islands will be free to-day,' and the ships did actually arrive in island waters that afternoon . . .

By early morning the town was alive – alive with a fervour never experienced before. People were arriving in St Peter Port from all parts of the Island – in motor-cars, petrol-driven converted tractors and on bicycles, and all wearing rosettes and bunting.

People, some utter strangers to each other, were to be seen shaking hands and congratulating themselves that they had managed to 'stick' it during the five long, weary years . . . Church bells, so long silent, pealed forth their joyous tidings of liberation, victory, and freedom.

At 7.14 a.m. Major-General Heine of the German Army signed the instrument of surrender aboard HMS *Bulldog*, and the Channel Islands were liberated. At 8 o'clock, the first British soldiers, twenty-two men of the

Royal Artillery, landed at St Peter Port, Guernsey, to take over an island with a German garrison of 10,000. They formed up on the docks, fixed bayonets and marched towards the dock gates.

The *Guernsey Weekly Press*:

The news that British troops had come spread around the island like a prairie fire, and within a very short time a vast crowd had gathered of cheering, weeping, delirious Islanders who gave these men of the British Army a welcome such as has never been equalled. As the troops emerged to cross the Esplanade, for the Royal Hotel, they were literally overwhelmed. Handshakes, embraces, kisses and back-slapping, mingled with fervent cries of 'Good old Tommies! Thank God you are here!'

The *Daily Herald* of 11 May reported:

Two girls with great Union Jacks led them into the town . . . The soldiers formed up each side of the old Courthouse steps on which the officers of the landing party and Victor Carey, Guernsey Bailiff, stood. Then the people sang 'God Save The King' with a sob in their throats, they looked up again, and cheered. That, to us all, seemed the real moment of the liberation . . . In the evening . . . Channel Islanders were cheering from motor-boats and rowing craft, and Allied aircraft were firing coloured lights which dropped green, red and violet over the freed and joyous Channel Isles.

Actually the Channel Islands were not yet completely 'free', it was not until the 16th that British troops landed on Alderney, taking the 3,200 German troops there prisoner.

The BBC Home Service radio programmes for that day included, after the 8.00 a.m. news, 'The Kitchen Front', a reminder that the war in Europe might be over, but rationing was not. At 9.45 to 10.05 there was Sandy Macpherson; this was most fitting. On the first few days of the war, back in September 1939, the scheduled programmes had been cancelled, to be replaced by official notices, sandwiched by what seemed like hours of Sandy Macpherson playing the organ, so it seemed right that he should also play the war out. Most of the rest of the day was taken up with popular music, including the John Watt Victory Party at 8.00 p.m., which was followed, at

9.00, by Big Ben, a minute for reflection, and the News and Victory Report.

Once again there were church services in most towns and villages that morning, Throughout the morning Churchill, as was his habit, worked in bed. In the afternoon, accompanied by his daughter Mary, he was driven in turn to the US, French, and Russian embassies, where toasts were drunk to victory.

A football match at Wembley, between a Combined Services team, and a National Police and Civil Defence side, scheduled for that day was re-designated an official VE Celebration. A large crowd watched the players, who included Marks and Bastin of Arsenal, Mortensen of Blackpool, Leslie

A Victory in Europe card from the RAF's 2nd Tactical Air Force.

Smith of Brentford, Burgess and Buckingham of Spurs, Goulden of West Ham, and Spence of Chelsea. There was cricket, too; the first Australian Imperial Forces side to play in London since 1919 took the field at the Dulwich Cricket Club ground in a one-day match against a Public School Wanderers XI. The AIF side, captained by the Test player A. Lindsay Hassett, included men who had fought in Greece, Crete, New Guinea, North Africa and Italy.

The afternoon was marked by street parties, mainly arranged with the children in mind. The *Liverpool Echo* reported that these parties often had a returned ex-prisoner of war or, failing that, a soldier on leave, as the special guest at the head of the table; for example, at the Sutton Estate, Gorton, Warrant Officer Harold West, having recently returned from two years in captivity, hoisted their Union flag.

Bessie Palmer remembered preparing for their party, 'I lived in this big block of flats and in the middle we had this square where the kids could play in safety, and out came all the tables.' Mrs Sewell recalled, 'We had a street party organised by one of the lady ARP wardens. I think we shared it with Lintaine Grove; they'd been bombed and half the street was gone.' Arnold Beardwell, 'We also went to a party at our local fire station, my dad was a part-time fireman.' Janet Houghton, 'We had a street party and someone had managed to get a piano outside, I couldn't believe it.' Alan Miles of Birmingham recalled his party, 'The whole road was turned into a party area, two or three radiograms at different points with the old 78 records, a piano, mouth organs, the old chap with a squeeze-box, and the party itself.'

Of course, as with all such parties, the central feature was the food. In *Westerham and Crockham Hill in the War* Helen Long recalled, 'I just remember that they did wonders with spam and fish-paste sandwiches spread about with a lot of green garnish. And there were jellies, too, in primary colours speckled with tinned fruit and decorated with frills of piped imitation cream.' Mrs Sewell, 'The whole street sat down to eat, the cakes and things were provided by the adults, it was marvellous when you think of the rationing.' Bessie Palmer remembered, 'Everybody was putting in something to make the party – we were still on rations – you didn't know what you were going to get to replace it. And the kids all went mad. Because we knew that it was over.' Alan Miles recalled:

Tables brought out and lined up, and covered with all manner of food, the likes of which we hadn't seen before, mostly home-made. Who could forget old Mrs Bent's blancmange and jellies, and 'pineapple chunks' – not really, they were diced swede soaked in sugar water and colouring, talk about improvising; and where did all the tins of meat, salmon, etc., come from? Not a lot was left I can tell you.

In Dulcie Grove, Levenshulme, Betty Griffiths sold raffle tickets to pay for their street party. The prize: two bananas – a very rare treat! In Didsbury, Herbert Mattison, a fruiterer in Didsbury Market, sent a large box of oranges for the Cross Street children's victory party.

Often, the meal was followed by street sports, with Savings Certificates the most common prizes. And there were other attractions; in Neath where a

Children's fancy-dress parade. Many local events and street parties included a fancy-dress competition for the children, similar to this one from Walthamstow.

by-election campaign was in progress, the Labour candidate, Mr D.J. Williams, took a loudspeaker van around the street parties, playing music for the children, and afterwards making a short speech to their parents!

Later, there were bonfires, as Alan Miles again recalled:

As soon as it started to get dark, with everything in full swing, the bonfire was lit; what made it special was the fact that two of our neighbours worked at the old Wilder's Firework Company, and did us proud with a cracking fireworks display. What a day – brilliant!

And, of course, it wasn't only the children having fun. Bessie Palmer remembered, 'Plenty of booze – I don't know where that came from. It was a feeling of relief, you let yourself go.'

The offices of the *Aberdeen Journal* bedecked with flags for the victory celebrations.

In Edinburgh there were similar scenes:

> The weather – bright sunshine and the mildest of breezes – was no doubt responsible for the thousands who made Princes Street Gardens their Mecca for the evening, when the thanksgiving service and concert at the Usher Hall was relayed from the Ross bandstand. Immediately after the proceedings at the Usher Hall had terminated, the loud speakers switched over to gay music, and until darkness the dance floor was packed.

That evening Churchill spoke once again from the balcony of the Ministry of Health:

> London, like a great rhinoceros, a great hippopotamus, said 'Let them do

their worst – London can take it.' London could take anything . . . never having failed in the long, monstrous days and in the long nights, black as hell.

Once again, there were large crowds out that evening. Field Marshal Brooke wrote in his diary that day, 'The majority of Englishmen apparently enjoy spending such a holiday by crowding together into the smallest space possible.' The *Glasgow Herald*, 'George Square, with its fairy lights and floodlighting attracted almost as large a crowd last night as on VE night itself.' The *Scotsman*, 'Big crowds were out again in Edinburgh on VE-Day + 1 – but there appeared to be a more subdued note about things.' The *Western Daily Press* told a similar story, 'Although thousands of people congregated at the Centre, Bristol, on Wednesday night to sing, cheer and dance, the crowds were slightly smaller than on VE night. On the other hand the suburban celebrations were more exuberant than ever.'

Of course not everyone took part in the revelry, as the *Scotsman* noted, 'Many have preferred to spend their Victory Days thinking their thoughts at home, tending the garden or listening to the broadcasts.' Yet revelry there was. The *Daily Sketch* commented, 'Those who thought the revels of Monday night might take the edge off the people's jubilation were proved laughably in the wrong.' But the party did not go on too late. As the *Western Daily Press* pointed out, 'By one a.m., however, Bristol was growing quieter. People were remembering that, for most of them, work began again next morning.'

And the evening had not been one of riotous drunkenness. In the area served by the Greenwich and Woolwich magistrates jurisdiction there was only one arrest for drunkenness, while in Glasgow, 'The whole scene was unspoiled by any scene of intemperance.' However, it was also reported that, over the holidays, the Cleansing Department of Glasgow Corporation collected almost three tons of empty bottles in the vicinity of George Square.

The war was, of course, not over; as Stevie Smith said, there was still Japan. But for the British public, a weight had been lifted, as Brian Martin remembered, 'It was a relief to go to bed and think that there would be no likelihood of German planes coming over looking for the local bomber aerodromes.' Joyce West agreed:

As I lived on the Downham Estate in Bromley, which was under the direct flight path of the bombers to London, school had been optional for any children who were not evacuated, and for those who came home between billet changes. It was wonderful to know that school would be open, and regular, once the war ended. It was a wonder that any of us passed our 11-plus that year, as we had had so many changes of home and school.

John Wheatley had other reasons to be glad. 'What a relief it was when the war finished and the lights came on again.' Peter Baker, 'So what did VE-Day mean to me? It meant that perhaps I could pursue a career without the thought of serving in the armed forces – little did I know that National Service would be introduced.' And of course, the 'Yanks' would no longer be 'over here'. Brian Martin, 'My wife remembers walking along the street in Diss at this time when a lorry load of American servicemen went by and shouted "Good-bye, you Goddamn Limeys".'

Alan Miles recalled the after-effects:

The aftermath wasn't so clever. It took a couple of days for the bonfire ash to cool down, and on clearing the debris it was found that the fire had burnt a hole about two-and-a-half yards square through the tarmac. The handful of cars in the road, and the bread and milk horse-and-cart had to go round the crater.

Immediately after the VE-Days were over the King and Queen began a series of visits around the country, starting with the East End of London on the morning of 10 May, while in the afternoon the royal couple and the princesses toured south-east London, their open-topped coach travelling down roads crowded with people. After a whistle-stop tour, on the 16th they were in Scotland, and next day they flew to Ulster for a two-day visit to the province.

'We may allow ourselves a brief period of rejoicing', the Prime Minister had said in his speech. Ideas of what constituted a 'brief period' varied. In the days following the VE celebrations, the BBC Home Service reflected the national mood. The holiday was over and, during the day, programmes were back to normal, The Kitchen Front was giving its usual advice at 8.00 a.m. to hard-pressed housewives, schools programmes were on, and for the workers there was 'Workers' Playtime' and 'Music While You Work', but in

Children, Union flags and ruined buildings – a scene from Battersea repeated up and down the country on VE-Day. *(IWM HU49414)*

the evening, victory celebrations continued. On Thursday 10 May, these included 'Victory Sing-Song' at 7.00, 'V-ITMA' at 8.30, and the Prime Minister at 9.00, followed by 'Victory Serenade – a programme of non-stop music'. Actually Churchill's piece was a long-arranged speech to mark his fifth anniversary as prime minister.

The pattern was followed all week, with, on Friday, 'Ulster Celebration' at 6.30 'a programme of thanksgiving from Northern Ireland', while at 8.30, headmaster Will Hay celebrated 'Victory at St Michael's' with his unruly pupils, who included Charles Hawtrey. At 10.15 there was 'Cap and Victory Bells', a celebration edition of the popular series, with Basil Radford and

Street parties sprang up everywhere as part of the victory celebrations. This is Lennox Road, Walthamstow.

Naunton Wayne. On Saturday there was the victory edition of 'In Town Tonight', and at 8.30, 'Victory Music Hall', featuring Josephine Baker, the Western Brothers, Issy Bonn and Ted Ray. On Sunday, of course, there were several victory thanksgiving services, including one broadcast from St Paul's at 2.45, attended by the King and Queen, and ministers of state.

It is interesting that the General Forces service had very little in the way of victory celebration programmes after the VE holiday. For many of its listeners the task at hand was still a serious one, and the time for celebration necessarily short.

Not all street parties took place during the two VE holidays. Doreen Last lived in Colchester:

Many roads in our area were arranging street parties in the days following and a group of teachers in our road was trying to get support for one on Saturday May 12th. However there was much controversy, particularly from two families, as a group of conscientious objectors refused to be called up and therefore survived, and on the other hand two families had lost their only sons in the war. Father would never tell us what happened, but the party took place at 5.30 on Saturday, with lots of food which everyone provided, and all the children were given ice cream. Then followed games and sports for all ages. I won the slow bicycle race and got a prize of 1 shilling! At dusk a huge bonfire was lit and we danced and sang 'til midnight, a rare treat after years of black-out.

Children's races were another part of most local parties and events. Here the winners are proudly showing off their prizes, which in many cases were sweets, or Savings Certificates.

Roy Wilcox lived in Bath:

Our playground at that time was a bombsite at the junction of Ringwood Road and Millmead Road, just a few yards from our house. The day after VE-Day we decided we would build a bonfire on the bombsite and started collecting the necessary wood etc. I told my father about this and later that evening and the following day he made us a 'Guy' with a face painted on an old tin with a Hitler moustache. My friend John decided that we should show the rest of our crowd our 'Hitler'. While we were showing off our guy, John was persuaded by a grown-up to go into the local pub (opposite the bombsite) to show it off to the regulars. To our surprise they made a collection and gave us the money to buy fireworks (which had just become available). We did not know what to do with this windfall. I told my father and he told me to leave it with him for a day or so. We continued building the bonfire.

My father then got together with friends and neighbours and organised a celebration for the following Saturday for the residents of Millmead Road, Ringwood Road, Lyndhurst Road and West Avenue, in the district of Oldfield Park. I strongly suspect that most of the planning was done at the local pub as word got round within hours.

There was to be a fancy-dress competition, parade and tea for children in the afternoon to be judged by 'senior' ladies, one from each of the roads. The money collected in the pub and other contributions were given as prizes.

In the evening there was to be an adults' fancy-dress competition. There was also to be dancing in the street and some households were asked if they would put a radio somewhere near the front door or window so that we could hear the dance music from the BBC. There was no street lighting at that time so electric light bulbs were put onto walking sticks and poked out of bedroom windows to give some light.

The next few days were very busy. Bunting went up across the roads. My mother made a banner to be carried at the parades, out of old black-out material with a pole at each end, and the words 'victory banner' sewn on it in white tape. We bought some fireworks for the evening. Fancy-dress clothes were thought up and made.

The great day arrived and all went well. The weather was fine; the parades and competitions were held and the whole neighbourhood came together to celebrate on or near the bombsite. When it became dark we set off the fireworks. We had placed Hitler on top of the public shelter in the street, and my friend John let off the first firework, which we had placed between Hitler's legs – you can imagine what it looked like, but we all laughed. After the fireworks were finished we danced and eventually put 'Hitler' on the bonfire.

I dressed up as Robin Hood, but my father gave strict instructions to the three lady judges that I was not allowed to be a winner, as he was one of the organisers.

There were a number of such small celebrations around the area, but there were several streets that missed out, so later on in the summer a large celebration was organised for the whole of Oldfield Park.

Peter J. Howell remembered:

I was six, approaching seven, and lived in Balsall Heath, Birmingham, in a long road of terraced houses, and there was a massive street party for the children. (My mother subsequently told me this was a week or fortnight after VE-Day.)

The whole street was festooned in bunting with Union Jacks and home-made decorations. My mother told me only a couple of years ago that, despite the rationing, everyone pulled together by pooling resources, a few spoonfuls of sugar here, a bit of butter there, so that we had jelly and blancmange and cakes. People somehow turned tables into benches or made tables from odd bits of wood.

After the party, games and races were organised the length of the road, other than the top end beyond the railway bridge where several houses had been bombed earlier in the war. My mother dressed me in a white sailor suit, a replica of a suit my father wore as part of a double comedy act and my fondest memory is of beating my best friend Harold in a fifty or hundred yard race up the middle of the road, even though I wasn't dressed for running. I kept looking back to see where Harold was and I can see my dad shouting 'Don't look back, keep on running!' I never won the race but beat my best pal which was pleasing enough.

**TRANSFORMATION SCENE BY T. ATKINS & CO.**

Cartoon from the *Liverpool Echo* of 7 May 1945 – T. Atkins is, of course, Tommy Atkins, the traditional name for the British private soldier, shown here being helped by Russian and American troops.

In the evening bonfires were lit every seventy yard or so, the embers of which did not die down until after we had gone to bed. We used any old sparklers we had. Given the constraints of the day everyone pulled together and put on a good party for us.

Besides the street sports, there were several 'victory' sports events arranged. Three one-day cricket matches were already planned between England and Australia, and it was quickly arranged to extend one of them to three days, to become the Victory Test Match. This was staged at Lord's, the first on the ground since 1939, and a crowd of 70,000 saw Australia win by six wickets. However it turned out to be only the first in a series of five Victory Tests. The second, at Sheffield, was won by England, the third, once again at Lord's, went to Australia, and the fourth was drawn. In the fifth and final Test at Manchester on 22 August, the series was levelled. An invitation cycling Victory Cup race was held on 2 June at the first Saturday meeting on the Herne Hill track since 1939. Also on 2 June, Northern League cup winners, Bolton, played Southern winners, Chelsea, in a victory celebration game which ended in a 2–2 draw.

Another traditional contest was being dusted off now that Germany had been defeated. On 11 May, the National Executive of the Labour Party issued its 'Victory Declaration'. Its central statement was, 'This war has been a People's War. The victory is, in very truth, a People's Victory.' After paying homage to all those involved in the fight, from commanders to rank-and-file and civilian workers, and offering sympathy for all those who had suffered loss, the declaration continued:

> With the war in Europe ended, and complete victory over Japan certain in the coming months, it now becomes the supreme task and duty of everyone to see that we win the Peace. There has been no faltering in our war efforts. There must be no faltering in our Peace efforts. Let us take heart for the future from what has gone before. The nation has shown courage, capacity and constancy in the fight to save freedom. It can be relied upon to display the same qualities in the fight to win prosperity, security and happiness.
>
> We salute the winning of victory in war. We call for the winning of victory in Peace.

On Sunday 13 May, called 'Thanksgiving Sunday', there were victory parades up and down the country, including in Birmingham, where the Lord Mayor took the salute of 16,000 representatives of the armed forces and civilian organisations, in front of over 100,000 spectators. Many of these local parades had originally been planned as VE-Day celebrations, but the sudden fall of Germany had meant that events had moved faster than local organisations could. The *Liverpool Echo* announced that, 'The official celebration of the day is to take place on Wednesday of next week [16 May] when a public parade of all the services will take place. It is probable that further festivities will be arranged.'

The *Kentish Mercury* reported:

Lewisham Borough Council, in common with other municipal authorities, had designed a VE-Day programme of celebration and thanksgiving, but notice was too brief to enable them to make the necessary arrangements to put the scheme into immediate operation. It was proposed to stage a pageant at the Gaumont Picture House on the first of the days appointed as a public holiday.

Many such local events were successfully converted into 'Thanksgiving Parades', and held that Sunday.

A flavour of the parades can be got from the programme of that of Bexleyheath, where the Thanksgiving Service was held in the Regal Cinema. The official programme includes:

The procession will assemble in columns of three in Highland Road, Bexleyheath, at 10.30 sharp, in the following order:-

North Kent Silver Band, Navy League Sea Cadet Corps, Girls' Naval Training Corps, an anti-aircraft unit, a searchlight unit, a US Army unit, cadets of the Queen's Own Royal West Kent Regiment, Air Training Corps, Girls' Training Corps, British Red Cross (men), British Red Cross (women), St John Ambulance (men), St John Ambulance (women), National Fire Service, Civil Defence Services, Women's Voluntary Service, Royal Navy Old Comrades, British Legion (men), British Legion (women), Home Guard Old Comrades' Association, Royal Air Forces Association, Boy Scouts, Girl Guides, Boys' Brigade (8th West Kent Regiment – Welling), Girl Campaigners, Royal National Lifeboat Institution, Rotary Club, Inner Wheel Club, Soroptimist Club, Chambers of Commerce, Burgesses of the Borough, Cottage Hospital Representatives, Bexley Local Savings Committee, Magistrates, National Association of Local

The celebrations picked up again on the weekend following VE-Day. The picture shows some of the vast crowd assembled in Union Street, Aberdeen, 15 May 1945.

Government Officers, Borough Officials, Councillors of Bexley, Aldermen of Bexley, Deputy Mayor of Bexley and Mayor's Chaplain, Mace Bearer, Mayor of Bexley and Town Clerk.

The Boys' Brigade will line the entrance to the Theatre and with the Church Wardens, will receive the Mayor . . .

When the head of the procession reaches the Theatre the first contingent will file off to the left-hand side of the road, the next contingent to the opposite side, and so on, each unit filing to the side of the road opposite the one immediately preceding it. The units will continue marching until the first one reaches the entrance to the Theatre when they will all halt and face inwards, thus lining the route to allow the Mayoral Party led by the Mayor in reverse order to proceed between the ranks into the Theatre, followed by the contingents in that order.

When the Congregation is seated the Colour Parties of all Organisations will form up at the main entrance and during the singing of the first hymn will proceed to the stage, where the Vicar will receive the Colours.

After the Service the Mayoral Party (i.e. all representatives in the Order of Procession from the Mayor of Bexley up to and including the Magistrates) will remain in the Theatre until the procession has been formed. The other contingents will leave the Theatre and will fall in outside in the original Order of Procession, led by the Band. The procession will be led back by the Mayor and the Mayoral Party. When the head of the procession has arrived opposite the Police Station, it will halt until the Mayor, the Council, and the Band have taken up position at the saluting base, when the procession will march past, the Mayor taking the salute.

At the conclusion of the march past, the National Anthem will be played.

John Wheatley remembered the parade in Torquay:

I was in the ATC brass band; a few days after VE-Day there was a sort of Victory/church parade at the local recreation ground with dignitaries taking the salute at a march past of local organisations. Our band played at several street and park victory parties that weekend.

Doreen Last took part in the parade in Colchester:

Next day, Sunday 13th May, I attended, with the Sea Rangers from Christchurch (off Malden Rd) the 'Victory Parade', meeting in Sheepen Road car park to march to Castle Park for a 3.00 service. There were very many local organisations in their entirety: forces, police, Home Guard, WVS, ARP, Civil Defence, nurses from the local military hospital, Army and Air Force Cadets, and many civilians. We then returned to North Hill for dismissal. There were thousands in the parade and still more thousands watching.

'Here you are! Don't lose it again!'

Philip Zec's cartoon from the *Daily Mirror* of 8 May summed up a concern for many amid all the rejoicing.

# CHAPTER 7

# *Aftermath*

Over the next weeks one of the first fruits of victory began to show itself. Brian Henderson witnessed one common scene:

> The troops were coming home, and while I was in Mapleton Road one day, I saw a soldier arrive home with his kit bag. Actually the soldier was Mr Mills, the father of Donald Mills, a boy in my class. As he stopped at the gate, and looked towards the house, his wife came from the side gate. They both hesitated for a moment, before hurrying to embrace. Realising this was a private moment, I looked away.

The men were coming home, and women were expected to look their best to greet them. *Vogue*'s 'Victory Number' suggested:

> Now I can find breathing space and can take time off for beauty once more. I must make haste to pick up any dropped beauty stitches, so that my beloved will not find me too much changed . . . I shall take not just one, but a course of Turkish baths and massage, to get the war right out of my pores.

The writer hoped that there would soon be lots of cosmetics available once again, but they were not available just yet:

> I shall sleek my eyebrows with castor oil, and brush up my lashes with it too, in the absence of mascara . . . I shall plunge my face into a basin of clear cold water every morning, opening and shutting my eyes whilst immersed, because this is a superb tonic for skin, facial muscles and tired eyes . . . I shall remember that, with evening dress again, my complexion starts much lower down, and I shall give my chest and back the same stimulating, nourishing care that I give my face.

Another *Vogue* article, on what was to be found in the shops, spoke of:

'[a] luxury . . . which will enchant a man home from the front, is a really lavish housecoat – essence of grace and femininity.' It went on to recommend, 'Jacqmar's Victory Scarf, for months a jealously guarded secret, is now revealed; a triumphant design of flowers and emblems in the colours of the United Nations, blazing on a ground of halcyon sky blue.' Alternatively, readers might wish to have their photographs taken 'for the soldier, sailor or airman who will like to have a present of your portrait to mark the summer of victory in Europe.'

On 29 May, Churchill told the House of Commons that 156,000 British and Commonwealth prisoners of war had been repatriated, while another 10,000 were awaiting repatriation in the British and US zones in Germany, 8,500 in Russian-controlled Austria, and 400 in Odessa. That same day, William Joyce, better known to millions in Britain as Lord Haw-Haw, was captured near the Danish–German frontier.

Welcome home! One of the immediate effects of the end of fighting was the return of the troops, a dream which most of them had had during the long years away. Some came back to a warm welcome, such as this greetings card suggests. For others, however, the reality was far removed from the dream.

All through May and June ceremonial disbandment parades of the civil defence services were held throughout the country. Typical was Bath, where the Mayor took the salute outside the guildhall, followed by a service at the abbey. On Sunday 10 June a farewell parade of representatives of all regions was held in Hyde Park, and was reviewed by the King.

Many large firms gave their workers a 'Victory Celebration'. Tarran Industries of Hull, for example, held theirs on 22 June. The celebration commenced at 6.00 p.m., at the Tivoli Theatre, with 'Frank E. Franks

As the end of the fighting in Europe was achieved, the troops began to come back. First came the liberated prisoners of war, to be followed by demobbed troops as, first the war in Europe, then in the Far East came to a conclusion.

Review – "Next Stop Japan"', followed at 8.30 by a dance and whist drive, at the Tarraneans Ground. The programme noted, 'While we cannot let up on our activity until the Japanese war is brought to a successful conclusion, we can celebrate the victory which has taken place. This is your night. Go to it and enjoy it.'

The end of the war in Europe brought to the forefront the arguments over the shape of post-war Britain. *Vogue* ran an interesting article entitled 'What We Want', which had three sections: to keep, to get rid of, and to have back. The 'to keep' section recognised that the war had brought some welcome changes. These included: the National Gallery lunch-time concerts, and the picture of the month at the same gallery (this was a system whereby one picture was featured each month, along with in-depth explanations and notes; this had been a good way round the fact that many of the paintings had been removed for their safety). 'Squares and gardens free of railings, decentralisation of cultural interests: concerts, London theatre productions, and travelling art exhibitions, moving around, not concentrated in the capital', day nurseries, 'bicycles, and some quiet roads on which to ride them', a basic food ration – 'the right of everyone to the elementary needs of life' and 'the black-out, one night a year, a night of full moon, to remind us of its beauty'.

The 'to get rid of' section (actually the shortest section), included, 'Ersatz' flavourings, watered-down beer, filling up forms, licensing laws, 'the chronic discomforts of travelling: every journey like a peace-time bank holiday, but without the fun at the other end', queues, identity cards, 'words like SEAC and UNIO which pepper the newspapers . . . Austerity – in its limited meaning of cramped dress restrictions, and in its larger meaning of a whole, thin-lipped attitude to life.'

The 'to have back' section included: 'our men and our children', sheer stockings, and 'wine, cheese, fruit, fruit and more fruit . . . lovely colours in fabrics, cosmetics, house paint . . . scarlet buses, scarlet fire engines', ice cream sundaes, perfume, fountain pens, elastic, four posts a day, restaurant cars on trains, lingerie with lace and frills, real sausages, late running buses and trains, nail varnish, combs and face cream, 'a sea view, uninterrupted by concrete blocks, barbed-wire entanglements or grand-stand scaffolding: and a free run of the cliffs and beaches without the danger of being blown up by a mine'.

**LOVE ME, LOVE MY DOG**

The dog in question is, of course, the Conservative Party. Churchill was hugely popular, but the Conservatives were not. Some even believed that Churchill would be asked to head a Labour Government, but the reality was demonstrated by this cartoon.

Some things were being got rid of; on 31 May, the last signs of shelters were removed from the London Underground; the final bunk of the twenty-six miles of triple bunks installed in the tunnels, and the last of the eighty underground medical-aid posts, were taken away. In all 1,500 tons of ARP equipment had been removed, including 125 shelter canteens and many shelter toilets.

Ironically, the outbreak of peace in Europe heralded an end to the political truce in Westminster. The issue on which the National Government would break up had first arisen early that year at the Reconstruction Committee – nationalisation of the electricity industry. The whole idea of peace-time nationalised industries was anathema to most Conservatives, whilst being close to the hearts of many in the Labour ranks. The arguments became increasingly bitter and personal.

Churchill tried to heal the wound, calling, on 18 May, on the Liberal and Labour Party leaders to keep the coalition government going until the defeat of Japan, or face an immediate election. The latter option was seen as bad for the 'opposition', as Churchill was still basking in a wave of post-victory public adulation, which would, the pundits averred, translate itself into Conservative votes. The National Executive of the Labour Party debated the proposal and, against the advice of Attlee and Bevin, rejected it, calling for an autumn election. Subsequently, on 23 May, Churchill resigned as leader of the coalition government, and formed a caretaker government of Conservatives, Liberals and non-party functionaries. At the same time it was announced that parliament would be dissolved on 15 June, and a general election called for 5 July.

Many believed that Churchill would easily win the election – Churchill mind, not the Conservatives – many saw it in those terms, and many Conservatives were happy to play that particular card. In this vein the Conservative manifesto was entitled 'Mr Churchill's Declaration of Policy to the Electors'. Labour, on the other hand, worked hard to establish themselves as the pragmatists who would lead Britain forward to the new post-war age, as opposed to the 'doctrinaire' Conservatives, who would take the country back to the grim days of the thirties. The Labour manifesto, 'Let Us Face the Future', promised to nationalise the Bank of England, fuel, power, iron and steel, and inland transport. Full employment would be maintained, and the schemes for a national health service, social security, and the new Education Act would be implemented in full. 'Mr Churchill's Declaration of Policy to the Electors' also promised to carry out many of the new social policies, but suffered from the fact that it was written in the stodgy style which the title suggests.

The actual campaign was far from staid. The Conservative line was that

Labour's ideas would inevitably lead to state control; this culminated in Churchill's infamous claim in an election broadcast of 4 June that the introduction of socialism would require some sort of Gestapo. Even at this stage most people saw Churchill as somehow above politics, and this plunge into the mud-slinging, yah-boo level of political 'debate' shocked and appalled many.

Although the election took place on 5 July, local holidays and the need to collect the votes of the many thousands of troops still stationed overseas meant that ballot boxes would not be opened until the 25th. When the results began to emerge, it soon became obvious that Labour had won by a landslide: 393 seats, against the Conservatives' 213, and the Liberals' 12. Churchill resigned and Clement Attlee formed a new, Labour, Government.

In fact, Churchill's 'Gestapo' folly probably had little effect. All opinion polls had shown the Conservatives trailing since 1943, while popular sentiment was for far more sweeping government controls than even Labour promised, such as the nationalisation of agricultural land. The nation was hungry for change and, after all, this was the first election for ten years.

John Wheatley recalled, 'I had no vision of a brave new world, but many had. There was lots of hope, promise and idealism. It was the servicemen thinking like this who put the Labour government into power; the only socialist government in our history. They had voted for a change.' Bryan Farmer remembered, 'Although Churchill had been a popular war leader, all the talk was about Labour coming into power, and nationalisation, a free health service and a country run for the people.'

Churchill had begun a meeting with President Truman and Marshal Stalin at Potsdam on the outskirts of Berlin on 17 July. On the 26th a proclamation was issued to the Japanese people, signed by Churchill and Truman (the Soviets were not yet at war with Japan), offering them the choice between unconditional surrender and annihilation. Two days later Prime Minister Attlee flew to Berlin with Foreign Secretary Ernest Bevin to take over at the head of the British team at Potsdam.

Throughout July the Japanese were being hammered. On 5 July General MacArthur announced that the entire Philippines had been liberated. Allied aircraft were now bombing Japan's cities almost daily, virtually without opposition, while on the 14th the Japanese mainland came under bombardment from Allied warships.

Late in the evening of 6 August, President Truman made the following announcement:

> Sixteen hours ago an American aeroplane dropped one bomb on Hiroshima, Japan. That bomb had more power than 20,000 tons of T.N.T. and more than 2,000 times the blast power of the British 'Grand Slam' which is the largest bomb yet used in the history of warfare.

Thus it was that the world learned of one of the war's greatest military secrets, the atomic bomb. Hiroshima had been virtually flattened. Of the population of about 330,000, official estimates put the death toll at 78,000, with 14,000 missing; and many more were to die over the coming months and years.

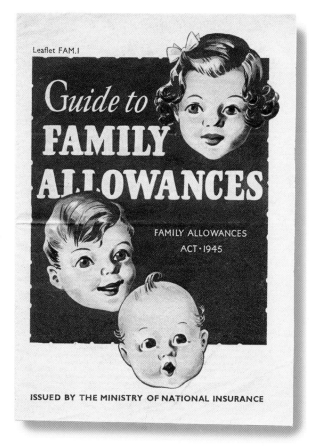

Leaflet FAM.I

Guide to FAMILY ALLOWANCES

FAMILY ALLOWANCES ACT · 1945

**ISSUED BY THE MINISTRY OF NATIONAL INSURANCE**

'Guide to Family Allowances'. The determination that the sufferings of the war had to be for more than just winning the war led to a series of social improvements.

In Britain reaction to the bomb was mixed. On the one hand many were appalled at the power of this new weapon – a feeling of vulnerability made all the keener after their first-hand experiences of the Blitz and the V-weapon assault. At the same time few condemned its use against Japan; after almost six years of conflict, there was little squeamishness left. The filmed revelations from Belsen and other concentration camps, seen by many at the cinema, and, more directly, stories of the harsh treatment, tortures and executions meted out by the Japanese against Allied prisoners, had many normal, decent people asserting that hanging really was too good for them – they should be tortured first. 'They', of course, referred to the leaders of the Axis forces, but six years of propaganda and the inevitable casualties of war, had led to a deep hatred of the enemy as a whole. People wanted the war over with as few Allied casualties as possible.

On 8 August, Russia declared war on Japan, beginning at midnight. At dawn on the 9th, Soviet forces attacked on a 1,000-mile front in Manchuria. Later the same day a second atomic bomb was dropped, this time on Nagasaki, and the results were equally appalling. A vast pillar of smoke rose from the stricken town which could be seen over 250 miles away. Soon after, Superfortress bombers dropped 3,000,000 leaflets on Japan calling for surrender before other atomic bombs were dropped.

On the 10th Tokyo radio announced that the Japanese government was prepared to accept the Allies' terms of surrender as set out at Potsdam, as long as the Emperor's sovereignty was retained. On the 11th US Secretary of State James Byrnes sent a message to the Japanese government via the Swiss legation in Washington. It was a rather ambiguous reply:

From the moment of surrender, the authority of the Emperor and the Japanese government to rule the State shall be subject to the Supreme Commander of the Allied Powers who will take such steps as he deems proper to effectuate the surrender terms. The Emperor will be required to authorise and ensure the signature by the government of Japan and Japanese Imperial General Headquarters of the surrender terms necessary to carry out the terms of the Potsdam declaration.

Meanwhile the Russian offensive in Manchuria was rolling on.

On the morning of Tuesday 14 August, the Japanese Cabinet met. There really was no alternative; they could no more stop the atom bombs than the British could have protected themselves from the V2s, the power of which had seemed so awful back in the autumn of 1944, but by comparison was a mere gnat's bite. They accepted the surrender terms dictated by the Allies.

At midnight, that night, Attlee broadcast to the nation, 'Japan has today surrendered. The last of our enemies is laid low.' He then read the Japanese reply to the Allied demands, ending with 'His Majesty [the Emperor] is also prepared to issue commands to the military, naval, and air forces of Japan, and all forces under their control wherever they may be found, to cease all active operations, relinquish all arms, and obey all commands of the Allied forces.' The Prime Minister then continued:

**Surrender – including face**

David Low's cartoon from the *Evening Standard* of 11 August. Throughout the war Low had produced many apt commentaries on the situation. Here he calls for the Japanese surrender to be truly unconditional, without any attempt to preserve 'face', or prestige and respect, among Japan's leaders.

Let us recall that on December 7, 1941, Japan, whose onslaught China had already resisted for over four years, fell upon the United States of America, who were then not at war, and upon ourselves, who were sorely pressed in our death struggles with Germany and Italy. Taking full advantage of surprise and treachery, Japan's forces quickly overran the territory of ourselves and our allies in the Far East, and at one time it appeared as though they might invade the mainland of Australia and advance into India.

But the tide turned; first slowly and then with ever-increasing speed and violence the mighty forces of the United States and the British

Commonwealth and Empire and all their allies, and finally of Russia, were brought to bear. Their resistance has everywhere now been broken.

At this time we should pay tribute to the men of this country, from the Dominions, from India, and the Colonies, to our fleets, armies, and air forces that have fought so well in the arduous campaign against Japan. Our gratitude goes to all our splendid allies . . .

We also think especially of the prisoners in Japanese hands, of our friends . . . in Burma and in those colonial territories upon whom the brunt of the Japanese attack fell. We rejoice that our sufferings will soon be at an end . . .

Here at home you have earned a short rest . . . I have no doubt that tomorrow and Thursday will be treated as days of holiday . . . Let all who can relax and enjoy themselves . . . Peace has once again come to the world.

The *Kentish Mercury* reported that, '[The] opening sentence of the Prime Minister's dramatic midnight broadcast on Tuesday was missed by many, but Mr Attlee's stirring message was not complete before the news of Japan's capitulation had spread as if by magic.' Fireworks, left over from VE-Day, or bought specially, and put away for just this occasion, began to be let off, lights went on, people came out into the streets, some in their slippers and dressing gowns. Many of those who lived near docks were awakened by the sound of hooters; at Gravesend a single ship started to sound its hooter, a call quickly taken up by others in a crescendo which lasted for two hours. Such scenes were replayed along many rivers. Some were woken by the sound, dimly took in that the war was over, then turned over and went back to sleep.

In *Bath at War*, David and Jonathan Falconer describe the scene in that city, typical of so many:

Huge crowds thronged Bath streets from shortly after midnight when the V-J news 'broke', until the early hours of this morning, singing, dancing and celebrating. Having heard the momentous announcement by the premier on the midnight news, people swarmed out of doors. Neighbours were hastily roused from sleep and scores of folk did not stop to dress – they just flung dressing gowns over their night attire and joined the

throng. A few minutes after midnight two Admiralty cars went screaming
through the city, their motor horns waking more and more people.

American soldiers had earlier come into Bath to spend the evening.
They were about to return to camp in two large lorries when the news
came. People climbed on to the lorries which made a tour of the city.

British servicemen joined arms and danced in the streets. Some of them
clanged salvage bin lids by way of accompaniment. Huge crowds marched
from the Guildhall up Milsom Street, where to their delight they were
showered with teleprinter punchings by postal workers on night shift. One
crowd went down Southgate street shouting, 'We want beer,' but all the
refreshment they could get was mineral water from the fountain at the end
of Bath Street. Someone with an accordion appeared and to the strains of
the music the people danced and sang and toasted each other in mineral
water.

Because of the late hour of the announcement, some people knew nothing
until the next morning. Typical was Mr W. Smith from Deptford who:

. . . got up as usual on Wednesday morning, peeped out of the front door
for a breath of fresh air, and saw a crowd of people at the end of the road.
I thought at first there had been an accident, but when I went along to the
corner, I found it was a bread queue.

Once again, the announcement of victory had been the signal for bread
queues. The *Scotsman* reported:

Even the early birds who set off before eight had to queue, . . . Those who
were later had a tough time. The shops were open all morning for the sale
of bread, fish, fruit and what not, but that was not to say you could buy
any. Orange peel lying about the streets suggested that some folk did get
oranges.

The following two days were declared public holidays. The official
programme included public thanksgiving services at Westminster Abbey at
10 a.m., noon, 3 p.m., 6 p.m., and 8 p.m., and at St Paul's Cathedral at
11 a.m., noon, 1 p.m., and 5 p.m. The bells of St Paul's would be rung
between 9 a.m. and 10 a.m., 11.30 and noon, and later in the afternoon

'Be funny if the siren went now, wouldn't it?'

Wild street scenes in London for the VJ celebrations, as envisaged by Giles in the *Sunday Express* of 19 August, though the policemen and some of those near them seem to be rather bored by the whole affair.

between 3.30 p.m. and 4 p.m., while the Westminster Abbey bells would also be rung at intervals throughout the day.

As it happened, that day had been marked down as the opening of the new Parliament. Just before the royal party was due to leave the palace to drive to Parliament, the persistent drizzle which had fallen all morning turned into a heavy downpour, but this did not deter the crowds. The King and Queen drove to the House in an open-topped coach through streets thronged with people, who by nine o'clock were lined six-deep behind a line of Guardsmen. The one sign that this was any different from the pre-war norm was the attending mounted guard, soldiers of the Household Cavalry, who were in khaki battledress instead of the usual ceremonial scarlet and blue. The King was in the uniform of an admiral of the fleet, with the Queen in 'her favourite light blue and furs'. As always Parliament was opened with the King's Speech, setting out the aims of his new government.

The surrender of Japan has brought to an end six years of warfare which has caused untold loss and misery to the world . . . It is the firm purpose of my government to work in the closest co-operation with the governments of my dominions and in concert with all peace-loving peoples to attain a world of freedom, peace and social justice so that the sacrifice of the war shall not have been in vain.

My government will take up with energy the tasks of reconverting energy from the purposes of war to those of peace, of expanding our export trade, and of securing by suitable control or by an extension of public ownership that our industries and services shall make their maximum contribution to the national well-being. The orderly solution of these difficult problems will require from all my people efforts comparable in intensity and public spirit to those which have brought us victory . . .

A measure will be laid before you to bring the Bank of England under public ownership. A bill will also be laid before you to nationalise the coal-mining industry. My ministers will organise the resources of the building and manufacturing industries in the most effective way to meet the housing and other essential building requirements of the nation . . . You will also be asked to approve measures to provide a comprehensive scheme of social insurance and to establish a national health service.

Once again, members of the House of Commons went in procession to St Margaret's Church, at 4 p.m., to huge cheers, especially for the new leader of the opposition, Winston Churchill. Members of the House of Lords, as before, went to Westminster Abbey, also watched by huge crowds. The *Scotsman* commented:

It was indeed an occasion when the weather did not appear to matter. Those who had come from early-forsaken beds to see the approach to Westminster were determined to stay for the return journey. By this time

# VJ

# Victory Celebrations

## ILLUMINATIONS

---

Wednesday, 15th August 1945.

and Thursday, 16th August 1945

SOUVENIR

# PROGRAMME

their ranks had been inflated considerably, and it was almost impossible to move except with the drifting crowds.

With the afternoon came glorious sunshine. On the whole the VJ celebrations would be a re-run of VE-Day. Once again thousands of people thronged The Mall and the approaches to Buckingham Palace, many of them scaling the base of the Victoria Memorial. They sang and shouted 'We want the King', and the King and Queen, accompanied by the princesses, responded by appearing on the balcony to be greeted with prolonged cheers. In all, the royal party appeared six times.

In Edinburgh:

A march by the pipe band of the Royal Scots was a lively interlude . . . behind the pipe band there marched a great swaying column. Soldiers, sailors, airmen, and civilians were linked arm-in-arm with girls and the efforts of some of the revellers to perform incidental fancy steps to the music of the pipes produced ragged, if comical effects.

Once again the King broadcast to the nation at 9.00 p.m.:

Three months have passed since I asked you to join with me in an act of thanksgiving for the defeat of Germany . . . I ask you again at this solemn hour to remember all who have laid down their lives and all who have endured the loss of those they love . . . Let us pray that one result of the defeat of Japan may be many happy reunions of those who have been long separated from each other . . . The war is over.

You know, I think that those four words have for the Queen and myself the same significance, simple yet immense, that they have for you. Our hearts are full to overflowing, as are your own . . . We have our part to play in restoring the shattered fabric of civilisation . . . It is to this great task that I call you now, and I know that I shall not call in vain.

Once again, principal buildings were floodlit from lighting-up time till midnight on both VJ-Days, though there were several more this time. In London they included: 'Buckingham Palace, Hampton Court Palace, the

*Opposite:* The cover of the leaflet setting out the programme of VJ-Day celebration events in London. Many local authorities published such leaflets.

Horse Guards, Shell-Mex House, the Houses of Parliament, Duck Island and bridge in St James's Park, the National Gallery, Nelson's Column, Somerset House, the Royal Mint, County Hall, Admiralty Arch, the Tower of London, the Royal Naval College at Greenwich, the Ministry of Health, St Paul's Cathedral, Middlesex Guildhall, Bethnal Green Museum and various municipal buildings.'

*Croydon and the Second World War* recounts:

Again the streets were beflagged and there were illuminations. Programmes of music were arranged in every part of the town, including a travelling band which played at various places on the outskirts. Music again was broadcast at intervals from the Town Hall. The sun, which had been obscured until 3 p.m., came out and Mayor Lewis again addressed the crowded audience from the balcony of the Town Hall . . . There was singing and dancing in Fairfield Car Park and the great bonfires on Duppas Hill, Addington Hills, New Addington and elsewhere continued into the night.

In Edinburgh:

The darkness relieved by lighted hotel and shop windows deepened as the evening advanced. Suddenly the Castle, floodlit, emerged from the darkened sky. The Nelson monument simultaneously stood out on the Calton Hill, and prominent buildings in the Old Town and Princes Street were also floodlit.

The *Birmingham Mail* of 16 August described the course of the festivities there:

The city had no organised plan of celebrations. The people celebrated victory according to their own desires, and that was why this day-long expression of joy was so successful and so spontaneous. From early morning thousands roamed up and down the main streets. Thoroughfares like New Street and Corporation Street carried thousands of folk bent on merriment.

It was a colourful picture. The early morning rain gave way to afternoon sunshine, and the folks then really 'went to town.' Scores came along in fancy-dress. There were impromptu concerts and dances in almost every

Like many other towns and cities, Aberdeen held a parade to mark victory against Japan on 'VJ-Sunday'.

side street, and Victoria Square, of course, was the main target area for Mr Brum and his large family. At one time there were over 30,000 people milling around, caught in the mad grip of delirious pleasure. The pent-up emotions of six years of war were let loose. 'Get it out of your system' seemed to be the general advice, and they did.

Once again there were bonfires. The *Mail* continued:

The youngsters had their celebrations nearer home. In many a side street there were afternoon tea-parties, and after dark leaping flames from thousands of bonfires cast grotesque shadows on the buildings around. It had been an all-day forage for fuel, and it was amazing to see what the folks really did burn – old furniture, mattresses, branches of trees and even garden gates and garage doors.

Elsewhere in Birmingham Alan Miles recalled that, 'Just for good measure, the residents of Dunsmore Road burnt another crater into the surface on VJ-Day!' The government wanted no repeat of the mass-burning of building materials that had taken place on VE-Day, and had broadcast an appeal not to do so on the 14th – to little effect

The *Western Daily Press* reported that:

Sailors in Colston Avenue started a bonfire of waste paper. They then rang for the fire brigade. When the NFS arrived in full force they were greeted with cheers from sailors desperately anxious to keep the fire going. One sailor stamped out the fire and then the whole crowd boarded the fire engine and departed in triumph for the fire station – for refreshments.

Once again, the beer ran out, as the *Western Daily Press* reported:

At Bathurst Basin, the older folk watched the fun from wooden benches placed strategically near a barrel of beer. In most other parts of the city beer was low, but spirits were high. Most of the public houses sold out early in the evening and the extension of hours was wasted. Nevertheless the good humour that was everywhere needed no stimulant.

The *Scotsman* reported that, 'Revelry continued far into the night and early morning. The Edinburgh Fire Brigade were called out to extinguish a few bonfires which were threatening property, but otherwise the night gave little trouble to the authorities.' Somebody did, however, set off a tear gas bomb in Princes Street in the late evening. No one was hurt, but several people had to put up with some discomfort, since, as the *Scotsman* put it, 'The habit of carrying gas masks was dropped a long time ago.'

News of the surrender had come rather more suddenly than expected and, as with VE-Day, the official plans for the festivities were left behind. However this time they were on the whole rather better prepared, and many celebrations took place on Thursday 16th, the second of the VJ-Days.

The *Kentish Mercury* of the 17th described the previous day's events in south-east London:

Yesterday's official celebrations began at 3 p.m. with 'Clown Bertram' at Middle Park School, Eltham, Punch and Judy at Avery Hill, and dancing at the Church Manor Way recreation ground, with the RA [Royal Artillery] Band at Plumstead Common. [There was] a football match between Charlton Athletic and the Woolwich team which is to visit Holland next month, and the festivities concluded with a firework display in front of the parade at Woolwich Common following music by the RA Boys band, and the RA Band.

As in the VE celebrations, VJ night saw bonfires and parties in many places throughout the country. This one is in Aberdeen.

For many in Britain these celebrations marked the end of a war which had lasted far longer than many had imagined possible in far-off 1939. Yet the VJ celebrations had for most been a pale imitation of those of VE-Day. The *Bath Chronicle* summed it up:

There seems no doubt in our minds that V-E was by far the better. Something seemed to be lacking in V-J. Maybe it was because it followed so soon (surprisingly) after V-E; maybe it was because people had been out in the early hours of V-J Day after the midnight announcement and let off a lot of their steam then; maybe it was because little time was given to make adequate arrangements for bunfights; maybe it was because V-E lifted the air-raid terror from us – there are lots of 'maybes'. At any rate, V-J night didn't provide the thrills of V-E. That's just our opinion, mark you.

The *Kentish Mercury* also noticed the difference:

A chat to a few neighbours made the answer clear. For most of the people of Deptford, Greenwich and Lewisham and neighbouring boroughs, the cessation of bombing with Victory in Europe was the end of their war. Not that they really forgot about the tremendous task our boys had to tackle in the Pacific areas, and there were still queues and other nuisances to suffer – but sudden death was no longer 'just round the corner'.

In fact Emperor Hirohito did not issue orders to his armed forces to lay down their arms until 16 August. On Sunday 2 September, almost exactly six years to the day after Neville Chamberlain had declared war on Germany, eleven representatives of the Japanese government signed the document of unconditional surrender aboard the battleship USS *Missouri* at anchor in Tokyo Bay.

The *Daily Mail* described the scene:

There was a lot of back-slapping and joking as on the deck below the ship's band played martial music.

Then – on the stroke of 8.30 – the deck was cleared, a crowd of Allied officers formed up in groups around the deck, and left in the middle was a small bare stretch for the surrender table and a microphone.

At this point a signal was sent to a destroyer upon which the Japanese delegates were waiting, that they should come alongside. The delegates slowly climbed to the deck. Before them, wearing no decorations, but just a plain khaki uniform and his well-worn campaign hat, stood General Douglas MacArthur, Supreme Allied Commander. He called them forward to sign the surrender document, and when it was over he dismissed them with scarcely a glance.

Actually, due to the nature of the areas occupied by Japanese forces, many did not surrender for some time afterwards; for example, the formal surrender of Japanese forces in Borneo did not take place until 10 September.

Reactions to the end of the war varied after the first explosion of relief and rejoicing. John Wheatley speaks for many who were in their teens at the time:

It might seem a wicked thing to say, but in a way I was sorry when the war ended. I was a schoolboy when it started until mid-1944 when I started work – it was an exciting time to be young; there was always something exciting happening. I joined the Air Training Corps in 1943 and thoroughly enjoyed every minute. Trips to airfields, camps and visits to other military establishments, in fact I remained in the ATC long after the war – all of the excitement of the military and none of the risk.

Patricia McGuire also had mixed feelings, 'My biggest regret was when the war finished. I was 12 years old and believe it or not I was upset because I wanted to join the Land Army.'

Those who thought that the end of the war meant the end of rationing and other restrictions were soon disillusioned as the reality of austerity Britain kicked in; on 1 September, it was announced that the clothing ration had been reduced by 25 per cent. Jenny D'Eath remembered, 'I was very disappointed that food shortages continued but in particular that sweet rationing continued.'

Bryan Farmer recalled:

The big disappointment for us youngsters who had grown up during the war was how long it took for everything to get back to normal, although we really couldn't remember what normal was. I remember the men in our

CITY OF PORTSMOUTH

# VICTORY CELEBRATIONS PROGRAMME

### SATURDAY, 8th JUNE, 1946.

# VICTORY MARCH

## FROM CLARENCE PIER TO SOUTH PARADE

VIA CLARENCE ESPLANADE

Commencing at 10.45 a.m.

......................................................

## ORDER OF MARCH

Mobile Column :

**ARMY TANKS**
**ROYAL MARINE MISCELLANEOUS VEHICLES**
**NATIONAL FIRE SERVICE VEHICLES**
**AMBULANCES**
**MOBILE CANTEENS & KITCHEN**

*PRICE - 3d.*

street coming home in dribs and drabs, unrecognisable from those who had left six years before. At our grammar school male teachers began to replace the women and parsons who had been drafted in 'for the duration'.

There were very few compensations in the immediate post-war period, but one stands out – the opportunity to go to the beach once again and enjoy outings to the local seaside resorts – though they were pretty rundown and the pre-war facilities took a long time to be up and running again.

Robb Wilton, the popular comedian, many of whose wartime stories had begun 'The day war broke out . . . ', did a radio sketch entitled 'The Day Peace Broke Out' in which he spoke for many when he said, 'There's nothing to look forward to now – there was always the all clear before.'

Because of the rather hurried official celebrations of VE- and VJ-Days, it was decided to hold a Victory Day on Saturday 8 June 1946. This time it was to be huge. In London the proceedings began with a royal procession, in which the royal family rode in a state landau from the Palace, along Oxford Street, then Charing Cross Road, to the saluting base in The Mall, arriving at about 11.00. There they joined Clement Attlee, Winston Churchill, and the prime ministers of several Commonwealth countries, who had themselves travelled there in carriages from Downing Street, arriving at about 10.30. The saluting base, which had been built especially for the occasion, was a sort of covered grandstand, in light blue and white, with a large royal coat of arms above it, surrounded by six masts from which were flown pennants bearing floral symbols of Great Britain and the Dominions. The seating on the base was strictly set out: the royal family on a raised dais in the centre, heads of government on their left, service leaders on their right, wartime ministers seated behind the royal family, with present ministers behind them, and members of the diplomatic corps on each side. The massed bands of the Guards were positioned opposite the saluting point.

Then followed a grand march past of, literally, thousands of troops, sailors and airmen, beginning with Allied contingents – including countries such as

*Opposite:* In June 1946, Britain celebrated its victories of the previous year with local parades, concerts, parties, and so on. This is the programme for the Portsmouth Victory Celebrations.

*"What was the post-war world like after the last war?"*

Cartoon by Giles from the *Daily Express* recalling the First World War poster, 'What did you do in the war, dad?' The talk of the period was all about the shape of the post-war world, and various people's plans for it.

Ethiopia, Iran, Greece and Luxembourg although, in a sign of the developing Cold War, Russia and Yugoslavia both refused to take part, and a Polish contingent was pulled out at the last minute. Next came Dominion and Commonwealth units, and lastly British troops and Home Guards. The march took a similar route to that of the royal procession, starting from Marble Arch, and finishing back at Hyde Park Corner.

There was also a mechanised column, made up of hundreds of vehicles from the forces, from tanks and self-propelled guns to motor-cycles, plus vehicles from the police, fire brigades, civil defence, the Women's Land Army (a tractor, of course), transport services and others. This went on a much larger route: from Regent's Park east to Cambridge Heath Road, south across Borough Bridge down to the Oval, west to Vauxhall Bridge, then north, via The Mall to Marble Arch and back to Regent's Park. There was also a fly-past which included Spitfires, Hurricanes, Lancasters, Mosquitos, and modern jets, Tempests and Meteors. Throughout the day there were many naval vessels, including submarines, moored on the Thames, which could be toured by the general public.

In the afternoon there was a whole series of entertainments planned in the main parks, Hyde Park, Green Park, St James's Park and Regent's Park, including orchestras and bands, community singing, a children's ballet, and folk dancing, Punch and Judy, and a performance of Shakespeare's *As You Like It*. After the great throng of the morning's parade, the park made for welcome family time. As *The Times* wrote, 'Hundreds of families, well provisioned with food baskets and carrying rugs and collapsible chairs, streamed on to the grass, well content, after sharing in the national ceremony, to spend an hour or two in the purely domestic pleasure of a picnic.' However, at about one o'clock it began to rain – people ran for the shelter of the trees, hoping it would pass, but by half past two it had become a downpour. Most of the afternoon's outside entertainments were cancelled, as the crowds, mostly dressed for a summer's afternoon, made for whatever cover they could find. Some events were hastily moved to indoor venues; the 200 children due to give the country dancing exhibition were given a party, and the promise that the display would be repeated later in the week.

As the evening approached the rain ceased, and events returned to plan. The royal party boarded their barge at Chelsea Bridge, from where they travelled in procession down the river to Waterloo before returning to Westminster and mooring at the Houses of Parliament, where they watched a huge water display, followed by fireworks.

Between Lambeth and Westminster Bridges, eight barges were moored on each side of the river, with a further five NFS fire boats in the centre, creating a sort of massive fountain effect, which was further enhanced with coloured lights playing on the water, smoke floats in the river, and flares dropped from aircraft. Many tourists had congregated in Trafalgar Square and Piccadilly, and the start of the fireworks signalled a general charge towards the river. The huge display commenced with a rocket barrage, and continued with set-piece displays opposite the Houses of Parliament, including 'portraits' of the King, Queen, and Princess Elizabeth. The whole thing finished with a salvo of magnesium shells which lit up the whole sky.

In the London suburbs, people cheered as the tanks and other vehicles made their way to and from the centre for the parade, then watched the flypast. In the afternoon, tea parties were the order of the day, quickly moved inside to schools, church halls, railway arches, or under tarpaulins. In the evening it was bonfire time again, with singing and dancing. Elsewhere, many cities had their own victory parades, and naval towns featured warships. In the towns and villages children's processions were the norm, with flags and bunting, and outdoor entertainment in the parks, not always cursed with rain, and everywhere there were street parties and bonfires and bands, even in those places which had decided, for whatever reason, against any official celebration. Millions followed the events in London on the radio, and, of course, a lucky few were able to watch the newly reintroduced television broadcast.

Brian Henderson remembered that:

> At school we received a personal illuminated message from King George VI, and we really felt the King had an affinity with us, because we had all been through the war. In the playground, a van arrived and showed a public information film. We were also given two sweets, boiled with soft centres.

Yet the hope for a new world began to fade with the bleakness of continued rationing and austerity. John Wheatley summed it up:

> In two or three years disillusionment set in. People were fed up with fuel and power shortages. The bad winter of '47 very nearly crippled the country. It was not only fuel shortages but general shortages – clothes, furniture, manufactured goods and luxuries. Petty-fogging regulations, bureaucracy, restrictions, forms in triplicate and permits. Maybe people expected too much too soon.

Bryan Farmer agreed:

> By the time I could vote it was evident it wasn't working quickly enough, the euphoria of victory soon subsided and a dissatisfied country reverted to Conservatism.

*Opposite:* Certificate from King George VI, issued to schoolchildren after the war. Many such certificates were issued to different civilian groups, people who had taken in evacuees, the Home Guard, and so on, recognising that this truly had been 'a people's war'.

DIEU ET MON DROIT

*8th June, 1946*

To-day, as we celebrate victory, I send this personal message to you and all other boys and girls at school. For you have shared in the hardships and dangers of a total war and you have shared no less in the triumph of the Allied Nations.

I know you will always feel proud to belong to a country which was capable of such supreme effort; proud, too, of parents and elder brothers and sisters who by their courage, endurance and enterprise brought victory. May these qualities be yours as you grow up and join in the common effort to establish among the nations of the world unity and peace.

*George R.I.*

# Acknowledgements

I would like to take this opportunity to thank the following people who so kindly shared their memories with me: Peter Baker, Arnold Beardwell, Jenny D'Eath, Bryan Farmer, Brian Henderson, Janet Houghton, Peter J. Howell, Muriel Jones, Doreen Last, Joan Letts, Patricia McGuire, Brian Martin, Alan Miles, Ken Moore, Sybil Morley, Bessie Palmer, George Pringle, Dorothy Richardson, Mrs Sewell, Joyce West, John Wheatley, and Roy Wilcox.

I would like to thank Her Majesty Queen for kindly allowing me to use the extract from the BBC documentary *The Way We Were*, first broadcast on 8 May 1985, and Sharon and Sean Kirk for allowing me to use excerpts from Leslie Kerridge's memoirs.

I should like to thank Josie Simons, who most kindly lent the photographs which appear on pages 141, 146 and 147, Froglets Publications which have kindly given permission to reproduce the photograph on page 137, and the Imperial War Museum, Wolverhampton Archives, Aberdeen Journals Ltd, Hull Local Studies Library, the *Hull Daily Mail* and Lewisham Local Studies Unit.

Finally I should like to give a big thank you to Carol, who gave me invaluable help with the illustrations.

# Bibliography

## Books

Anon, *BBC War Report*, Oxford University Press, 1946

Anon, *BBC Year Book 1945*, BBC, 1945

Anon, *Croydon and the Second World War*, Croydon Corporation, 1949

Anon, *London Transport Carried On*, LTPB, 1947

Addison, Paul, *The Road to 1945*, Jonathan Cape, 1975

Blake, Lewis, *Bolts from the Blue*, Lewis Blake, 1990

Collier, Richard, *The City That Wouldn't Die*, Collins, 1959

Falconer, David and Jonathan, *Bath at War*, Sutton, 1999

Fleming, Peter, *Invasion 1940*, Hart-Davis, 1957

von Kardoff, Ursula, *Diary of a Nightmare*, Hart-Davis, 1965

Kiesler, Egbert, *Hitler on the Doorstep*, Arms & Armour Press, 1997

Lukacs, John, *Five Days in London*, Yale Nota Bene, 2001

Maurois, André, *Why France Fell*, Bodley Head, 1941

Ogley, Bob, *Doodlebugs and Rockets*, Froglets, 1992

Sansom, William, *Westminster at War*, Faber & Faber, 1947

Skidelsky, Robert, *Oswald Mosley*, Macmillan, 1981


## Pamphlets

*Women and the Peace*, Conservative Party pamphlet, 1945

## Periodicals

*Cleveland Evening Gazette*

*Daily Express*

*Daily Herald*

*Daily Mail*

*Daily Mirror*

*Daily Sketch*

*Daily Telegraph*

*Evening News*

*Glasgow Herald*

*Guernsey Weekly Press*

*Kentish Mercury*

*Liverpool Daily Echo*

*Manchester City News*

*News Chronicle*

*Picture Post*

*Radio Times*

*Scotsman*

*The Times*

*Vogue*

*War Weekly*

*Western Daily Press*

*Wolverhampton Express & Star*

# Index